Knowing Our Catholic Faith

Beliefs and Traditions Worktext

Level Eight

Loyola Press

Nihil Obstat: Michael Cameron, Ph.D.
                  Censor Deputatus
                  March 21, 1999

Imprimatur: Most Reverend Raymond E. Goedert, M.A., S.T.L., J.C.L.
                  Vicar General
                  Archdiocese of Chicago
                  March 25, 1999

Acknowledgments:
The Scripture quotations contained herein are from the *New Revised Standard Version Bible*, Catholic edition, copyright © 1993 and 1989 by the Division of Christian Education of the National Council of the Churches of Christ in the U.S.A. Used by permission. All rights reserved.

English translation of the *Catechism of the Catholic Church* for the United States of America, copyright © 1994, United States Catholic Conference, Inc.—Libreria Editrice Vaticana.

English translation of The Canticle of Zechariah and The Magnificat by the International Consultation on English Texts.

(Acknowledgments continued on the inside back cover.)

Editors: Amy Joyce, Anna Urosevich, Pedro A. Vélez

Cover Design: Jennifer Carney

Production: Genevieve Kelley, Molly O'Halloran, Jill Smith, Leslie Uriss

 Loyola Press

3441 North Ashland Avenue
Chicago, IL 60657
1-800-621-1008

ISBN: 0-8294-1137-2

00   01   02   03   04   5   4   3   2

Knowing Our Catholic Faith

Beliefs and Traditions Worktext

Level Eight

Author
Peg Bowman

Consulting Author
Mary K. Yager

Principal Program Consultants
Sister Kathryn Ann Connelly, S.C.
Most Reverend Sylvester D. Ryan, D.D.
Reverend Richard Walsh
Jacquelyne M. Witter

 Loyola Press

Contents

My name is _____.

I am a member of the Catholic Church.

My parish is _____ in _____.

This is a review of the doctrines of the Catholic faith, based on the teachings in the *Catechism of the Catholic Church.* This book covers what we Catholics believe, how we celebrate, how we live our faith, and how we pray. The *Catechism* will be an important reference book for you soon, and this review text already includes many quotations from it. If you can, look at a copy of the *Catechism* itself to give you an idea of all it covers.

The written activities after each lesson are intended to help you remember the doctrines that are taught. You can read the book and do the activities alone or with a friend or family member or in a religion class. You will also need a Bible to complete some of the activities.

Section One
Our Catholic Beliefs

The first part of the *Catechism of the Catholic Church,* titled "The Profession of Faith," is based on the articles of faith found in the Apostles' Creed. The following fourteen lessons provide a summary of much of the material from this first part.

As you read this section and complete these activities, you will notice that some of this material is a review for you. Pay attention, however, to the new material included, too. It is all designed to help you increase your knowledge of the basic doctrines of the Catholic faith.

How God Is Revealed

Catechism paragraphs 50–55, 68–70

Early in the *Catechism* there is the following statement: "The desire for God is written in the human heart, because man is created by God and for God; and God never ceases to draw man to himself" (paragraph 27).

Take a few minutes to think about this. Can you see what is written in your heart?

God has made us to know him, and on our own we would at least know that God exists, that there is someone greater than we who brought everything into being. God knows the questions we have about him and about the meaning of life. He knows our restlessness and our desires. In his great love, God has a divine plan of **revelation.** He wants to communicate himself to us so that we can know him, love him, and serve him.

Revelation has taken place gradually as God has revealed himself in stages over thousands of years. The earliest revelations are reported to us in the **Old Testament** of sacred Scripture. All those early stages of divine revelation were preparing the people for the final, full revelation: Jesus **Christ,** the Son of God.

There will be no more new public revelations, *but there continue to be new people to whom God will reveal himself.* Each of us are among these new people. God has been revealing himself to you for many, many years, but now that you are older you might be ready for more revelations. Are you ready to read the revelations from Scripture with new eyes? Are you ready to listen to the revelations of Jesus in the Gospels with new ears? Can you hear the revelations God sends through the Church?

God is calling you to know, love, and serve him. Can you hear?

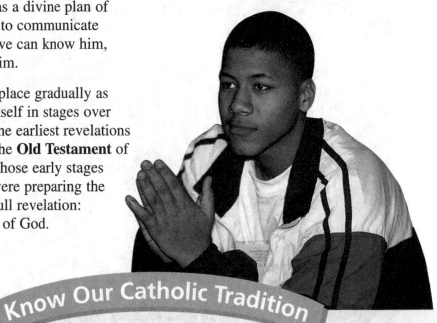

Know Our Catholic Tradition

St. Augustine wrote, "Our hearts are restless until they rest in you, O God" (*Confessions,* Book I). Do you ever feel restless? Do ever want something beyond your reach? Could it be that you and other people your age are restless for God like St. Augustine suggests? Wise men and women for centuries have reported—often first when they were your age—this restlessness and this desire. They have also *identified* what it means: Human beings by our nature long for God and search for meaning in our lives.

A Prayer in Response to God

Use the sentence starters below to write a response to God for calling you to salvation. Use your own words to write your sincere thoughts.

God, I believe the desire for you is written in my heart. You know I've been restless

lately. I've been most restless _____

_____

_____.

Here are some things I want that seem to be beyond my reach: _____

_____

_____.

God, I have questions about you. I wonder _____

_____

_____.

God, I know you've already revealed some things to me about yourself. These are

some things I know about you: _____

_____

_____.

God I ask that _____

_____

_____

and I thank you for _____

_____

_____.

One God, Three Persons

Catechism paragraphs 230–267

Some of the truths of our faith are **mysteries of faith**—truths that cannot be discovered by human thought alone. These mysteries are revealed to us by God through the words of Scripture, through Jesus, and through the teachings of the Church.

Do you remember which mystery the *Catechism* calls the *"central mystery of our faith"* (paragraph 234)? It is the mystery of the most **Holy Trinity.** God has revealed this about himself: There are

three persons in the one true God. They are God the **Father,** God the **Son,** and God the **Holy Spirit.** It is central to our Catholic faith that we believe there is only one God, yet we also believe God is three persons!

Each person of the Blessed Trinity has a different mission, yet we know that they are not separated as they carry out these missions.

God the Father's mission is *creation.* Everything exists because of him. Jesus revealed, however, that we should also call God "Father" because he is a loving parent who cares for all his children.

God the Son's mission is *salvation;* he is our *Savior.* He was part of the Trinity from all eternity, but at a moment in time he became human, lived on earth to teach us how to live, and died to save us from our sins.

God the Holy Spirit's mission is to *make us holy;* he is our **Sanctifier.** The Spirit sanctifies us by filling our souls with **grace.** It is the Holy Spirit who inspires all good thoughts, actions, and prayers.

Our belief in the Unity and Trinity of God is the most basic belief of our faith.

Know Our Catholic Belief

We begin our prayers by calling to mind the Trinity when we pray,
"In the name of the Father and of the Son and of the Holy Spirit."
We end many prayers by remembering that we pray
to the Father, through Jesus Christ the Son, in the unity of the Holy Spirit.

Clues and Transfers

Fill in each blank below. When a line has a number beneath it, transfer that letter to the blank marked with that number at the bottom of the page. When you are finished, the transfers will spell an important message.

1. The central mystery of our faith is the mystery of the

    __ __ __ __   __ __ __ __   __ __ __ __ __ __ __ .
    6 22 29 15   18   17 8 23   21

2. The three persons in one __ __ __ cannot be __ __ __ __ __ __ __ __ __ __.
                            1   28   10 16   11 27 7   3

3. We also call the Holy Trinity the __ __ __ __ __ __ __ Trinity.
                                     19   5 14   24

4. Each person of the Trinity has a __ __ __ __ __ __ __ .
                                    12   26 9

5. The Third Person of the Trinity makes us __ __ __ __ .
                                             2   13

6. God the Son lived on __ __ __ __ __ to teach us __ __ __ to live.
                        20   4   25

THE MESSAGE:

__ __ __   __ __ __ __ __ __ __   __   __ __ __ __ __ __ __
 1 2 3   4 5 6 7 8 9 10   11   12 13 14 15 16 17 18

__ __ __ __ __ __   __ __ __ __ __.
19 20 21 22 23 24   25 26 27 28 29

Created in God's Image

Catechism paragraphs 355–384

In your science classes you've probably studied several theories about how the universe began. You've learned of evidence proving the universe has been in existence for billions of years. Perhaps you have wondered how these scientific facts and the stories about creation in the Bible could both be true.

We Catholics understand that *both* scientific knowledge *and* Bible teaching are true!

The human authors of Scripture lived at a time when knowledge of the earth was not very accurate. Inspired by God, they wrote the *religious truths* of Scripture. It was not their goal to write scientific truths. The

religious truth that God created the universe by his own power, out of nothing, is repeated in several different creation stories in the Old Testament.

The most familiar of these are the two stories in Genesis 1—2:3 and Genesis 2:4–25. There is also Psalm 104 about how God created the world. The longest and most fantastic description of creation is in Job 38—39.

Can you recognize the religious truths these stories teach us?

- God alone created everything out of nothing.
- Everything God created is good and is part of an orderly plan.
- God created human beings in his own image to care for the earth and all its creatures.

What about science? The more we learn from science about how complex creation is, the more we can praise God for all he has made. The *Catechism* tells us to thank God "for all his works and for the understanding and wisdom he gives to scholars and researchers" (paragraph 283).

Know Our Catholic Belief

God has made us **stewards** of the earth. A steward is a trusted servant who cares for another person's property. We recognize that everything belongs to God and comes from God. It is up to us, however, to use the grace of Jesus' salvation not only for ourselves but for our fragile earth!

Crossword Puzzle

As you learned in this lesson, Scripture contains several different descriptions of how God created the world. Use your Bible to complete this crossword puzzle.

ACROSS

2. In Job 38, what does God keep in a storehouse?
5. In Genesis 2, what did God plant in Eden?
6. In Psalm 104, God travels on the wings of the _____.
8. In Psalm 104, what fled from the sound of God's roaring thunder?
10. In Genesis 2, who did God create to be a companion to man?
11. In Psalm 104, what animals take refuge in the rocks?
14. In Psalm 104, all of creation is dismayed when God hides his _____.
16. In Job 38, God calls the clouds the earth's _____.
17. In Genesis 2, this is the day God rested.

DOWN

1. In Genesis 1, what did God call all he had made?
3. In Psalm 104, all is created when God sends forth his _____.
4. In Genesis 2, the man could not eat from the tree of _____.
7. In Genesis 1, what did God place in the middle of the waters to separate them?
9. In Psalm 104, what did God make the moon to mark?
10. In Job 38, who does God shake from the surface of the earth?
12. In Genesis 1, what did God create first?
13. In Genesis 2, what did man give to all the animals?
15. In Psalm 104, what did God give us to "gladden the human heart"?

The Incarnation

Catechism paragraphs 422–483, 512–534, 561–564

The mystery of the **Incarnation** teaches that the *Son of God became human.*

Why did God do such a thing? Why was God willing to become human? The only explanation is *love.* This plan, for God to become human, was the only way God could save us from our sins.

We were made in God's image, but we had lost our likeness to God through sin. Now, God came to live as a human so that we could regain our likeness to God. God loves us that much!

It is important to remember that Jesus is truly God and also truly human. He was not a God pretending to be human, and he was not a human pretending to be God. He was able to take on our human nature without losing his divine nature. In this way he could be the mediator between God and all of humanity.

Each of us has only one nature, our human nature. Jesus has two natures: his divine nature and his human nature. The Incarnation is the mystery of the union of these two natures. Fully human, Jesus could experience all the experiences of human nature. The Gospels tell us of his hunger and thirst, his weariness and anger, his sorrow and pain. He became like us in everything except sin.

The Church teaches that Jesus did this for *each one* of us individually! We can hardly imagine so much love. We cannot imagine being worth so much. When you look at a picture of the infant Jesus in the stable or at a crucifix showing the suffering Jesus, try saying this: "Jesus did this for *me.*"

Remember that the Book of Genesis tells us first that God made us in his own image, then later that our first parents lost all of that by their disobedience. Here is what the Incarnation means to us: Jesus gave us back our dignity. We are once again able to live in God's image.

Know Our Catholic Belief

Here is how the Nicene Creed describes Jesus' divinity:

"We believe in one Lord, Jesus Christ, the only Son of God,
eternally begotten of the Father,
God from God, Light from Light,
true God from true God,
begotten, not made, one in being with the Father.
Through him all things were made."

Word Search

Answer the questions below, and search for them in the puzzle grid. When you have circled all the words, the remaining letters, written in order, will spell a hidden message.

```
E  N  I  V  I  D  P  I  X  O  L
N  E  A  C  H  A  B  M  I  R  O
L  Y  V  S  R  O  E  A  I  E  V
S  I  S  E  N  E  G  G  F  H  E
I  N  N  O  R  F  O  E  C  T  N
N  T  R  U  L  Y  T  G  U  A  I
S  M  E  D  I  A  T  O  R  F  G
O  N  I  C  E  N  E  H  C  D  A
O  W  T  Y  T  I  N  G  I  D  M
N  O  I  T  A  N  R  A  C  N  I
M  A  D  E  S  L  E  P  S  O  G
```

1. Jesus is "eternally _____ of the Father."
2. When we look at a _____ showing Jesus suffering, we remember he died for us.
3. Jesus gave us back our _____.
4. Jesus is God, so he has a _____ nature.
5. Jesus became human to save _____ one of us.
6. Jesus became like us in _____ except sin.
7. Jesus is "one in being with the _____."
8. The Book of _____ teaches us God made us.
9. The _____ tell us of Jesus' human experiences.
10. We were made in God's _____.
11. We can hardly _____ so much love as the love Jesus has for us.
12. The _____ is the mystery that God became human.
13. _____ is the reason the Son of God was willing to become human.
14. Through Jesus "all things were _____."
15. Jesus is the _____ between God and all of humanity.
16. We read a description of God's divinity in the _____ Creed.
17. By the disobedience of our first _____, we lost our likeness to God.
18. Jesus became human to save us from our _____.
19. Jesus is _____ God and _____ human.
20. Jesus has _____ natures.

HIDDEN MESSAGE:

_____.

The Covenant Stories

Catechism paragraphs 50–73

The **covenant** stories reveal, step-by-step, God's plan to save us from the power of death. We find the earliest covenant in the Book of Genesis. After the great flood, God made a covenant with Noah, saying: "I establish my covenant with you, that never again shall all flesh be cut off by the waters of a flood, and never again shall there be a flood to destroy the earth" (Genesis 9:11). God has made it clear that he wants humanity not to die but to live.

In the next covenant God begins to form a people for himself. Abraham, Sarah, and all their descendants became God's chosen people. God promised them, "I will establish my covenant between me and you, and your offspring after you throughout their generations, for an everlasting covenant" (Genesis 17:7).

Before that covenant could be fulfilled, however, more preparation and revelation were needed. God raised up the great leader Moses to lead the Israelites out of slavery in Egypt. On their journey they, too, were offered a covenant with God. He said to them, "I will walk among you, and will be your God, and you shall be my people" (Leviticus 26:12). With that covenant God gave them the Law. He wrote the commandments on tablets of stone.

What was all this leading up to? For centuries, prophets spoke and wrote about a promised **Messiah.** For example, Isaiah wrote, "For a child has been born for us, a son given to us; authority rests upon his shoulders; and he is named Wonderful Counselor, Mighty God, Everlasting Father, Prince of Peace" (Isaiah 9:6).

Then came a prophecy in which God reveals much more of his plan. Jeremiah wrote:

> The days are surely coming, says the Lord, when I will make a new covenant with the house of Israel. . . : *I will put my Law within them, and I will write it on their hearts;* and I will be their God, and they shall be my people.
> Jeremiah 31:31, 33

No longer would the Law be written on tablets of stone. It would be in our hearts. It would become a Law of love, not of fear; a Law of freedom, not of slavery to sin. How would this come about?

At last, God the Father sent his Son, Jesus, to establish his final covenant. No more covenants will be offered. No more revelation will be needed. Jesus has fulfilled all God's promises. We are saved in the waters of **Baptism**—not destroyed by the flood. We are part of a "nation" of people, the Church, blessed in Christ.

Know Our Catholic Belief

In Christ the Law given to Moses is written in our hearts.
Jesus did not come to destroy the Law or even change the Law.
The Son of God became human to fulfill the Law and to set us free.

Prophecies about the Messiah

Use your Bible to find the passages below. Then decide which phrase at the right best fits each passage and write the correct letter on the line in front of the passage.

1. ___ Zephaniah 3:15-20

2. ___ Genesis 3:15

3. ___ Isaiah 53:1-7

4. ___ Micah 5:1

5. ___ Isaiah 11:1

6. ___ Malachi 3:1-2

7. ___ Isaiah 7:14

8. ___ Jeremiah 31:31-33

9. ___ Isaiah 9:6

A. He shall be from Jesse's family.

B. His mother will be a virgin.

C. He will be a king sitting on David's throne.

D. He will step on the head of the snake, Satan.

E. He will save Jerusalem and joyfully bring her people home.

F. He will make a new covenant of love with us.

G. He will be born in Bethlehem.

H. He will have a messenger come before him.

I. He will suffer and die for us.

Jesus' Death

Catechism paragraphs 571–573, 610–612, 620–621, 624–627, 638–647

We recall Jesus' suffering and death at each **Eucharist**, and the Church sets aside one week each year, Holy Week, to reflect more carefully on the **Paschal mystery**. Most Catholics try to participate in most or all of the liturgies of Holy Week.

Holy Week begins on Palm Sunday when we hear the story of Jesus' entry into Jerusalem while a crowd welcomed him, waving palm branches and cheering "Hosanna!" On that same Sunday we also hear a reading of one of the Gospel narratives of the Passion. We are faced with the sad truth—the same crowd of people shouted "Hosanna" on Sunday and "Crucify him" on Friday. *Are we ever like that crowd of people?* Palm Sunday is a day to admit we are and to ask God for forgiveness.

On Holy Thursday we follow Jesus and his apostles to their **seder** meal for the Jewish Feast of Passover, Jesus' last supper. We reflect on many things this day. We hear the story of Jesus washing the feet of his apostles (John 13:3-15), and we hear Jesus command, "If I, your Lord and teacher, have washed your feet, you also ought to wash one another's feet" (John 13:14). *Are we supposed to serve others, too? How?*

During the meal he blessed bread and wine and said, "This is my body. This is my blood. Do this in memory of me." He gave us the Eucharist. He gave us himself. *Are we worthy to receive this gift?* After the meal, we follow him to the Garden of Olives. We hear Jesus ask his disciples to pray with him for an hour. *How often do we really spend time with Jesus?*

We call the next day Good Friday. For Christians, it is a very quiet day. Our **tabernacles** are empty. No Masses are celebrated. Instead, we gather to remember how Jesus suffered and died. We hold his cross on high and venerate it because for us the cross is an instrument of salvation.

Jesus, though, *was* tortured. Jesus did wear a crown of sharp thorns. Jesus was beaten and spit upon and mocked. The cross was an instrument of torture for him.

What can we say to him now? What can we say to him for doing all this for us?

Know Our Catholic Tradition

"Let us proclaim the mystery of faith!" the celebrant invites us at each Eucharistic Liturgy. We reply by announcing the Paschal mystery: "Christ has died, Christ is risen, Christ will come again!"

You Are There

Use your Bible to read about each scene below. Imagine who you might have been in the scene and then write a prayer to Jesus about your thoughts and feelings.

Matthew 21:1–11
Jesus, if I had been there,
I think I would have been_____.

Jesus, I want to say _____

_____

_____

_____

_____

_____.

_____

Mark 14:32–42
Jesus, if I had been there,
I think I would have been_____.

Jesus, I want to say _____

_____

_____

_____

_____

_____

_____.

Luke 23:1–56
Jesus, if I had been there,
I think I would have been_____.

Jesus, I want to say _____

_____

_____

_____

_____

_____.

John 13:3–15
Jesus, if I had been there,
I think I would have been_____.

Jesus, I want to say _____

_____

_____

_____

_____

_____.

_____

Catechism paragraphs 638–667

The culmination of Holy Week and of the Church year is Holy Saturday. There are no services in our churches that day. When we arrive for the Eucharistic Liturgy that night, we find the church as dark as a tomb.

A new fire is lit. That fire is used to light a large Paschal candle. A **deacon** proclaims: "Light of Christ!" as the candle is carried through the church. Now there is a strong flame to pierce the darkness in our church building.

Often small candles are lit from the Paschal candle. Points of flame shine all over the building as we see the new candle plunged into the water that will be used for Baptism, and as we hear the joyful singing of an ancient song of Easter praise called the **"Exsultet."**

When we finally hear the proclamation of the Easter Gospel, the amazing story of the empty tomb, the running apostles, the excited women, the risen Jesus— we fill our churches with joyful music and lights and flowers. Alleluias fill the air.

New Christians are born in our churches on Holy Saturday night. People who have been preparing for months now are baptized and confirmed. We who were already baptized stand with them and

renew our **baptismal promises.** We are one family of faith believing in one risen Lord and one Baptism!

Easter is too important to fit into one day. The Church celebrates Easter for seven weeks. During that time, we hear stories of the time after the **Resurrection** when Jesus appeared to many of his disciples. We continue to sing hymns of Easter joy and to enjoy the new life of Baptism and of spring.

Then, 40 days after Easter, we celebrate the Feast of the **Ascension.** Jesus couldn't stay with the disciples. He ascended into **heaven** to be with his Father. Before he left, however, he promised to send the Holy Spirit (Acts 1:6-11).

Know Our Catholic Belief

The Scripture stories on Holy Saturday night remind us that all the promises "both of the Old Testament and of Jesus himself" have been fulfilled this night. All the covenants have been kept (*Catechism,* paragraph 652).

Who Did That?

Use Matthew 28, Mark 16, Luke 24, and John 20 and 21 to match the people listed in the column on the right with the actions in the column on the left. Be careful! Some names will be used more than once and some not at all.

___ 1. Rolled back the stone and sat on it.

___ 2. Became like dead men.

___ 3. Bribed the soldiers to say Jesus' body was stolen.

___ 4. Went with Mary the mother of James and Salome to bring spices to the tomb.

___ 5. Met the women running from the tomb, greeted them, and told them what to say.

___ 6. Left the tomb and said nothing to anyone.

___ 7. Scolded the apostles for their unbelief.

___ 8. Thought the women were talking nonsense.

___ 9. Met Jesus on the road to Emmaus.

___10. Revealed himself in the breaking of bread.

___11. Ate a piece of baked fish.

___12. Thought Jesus was the gardener.

___13. Raced to the tomb with Peter and got there first.

___14. Wouldn't believe in the risen Jesus unless he could touch his wounds.

___15. Jumped into the sea to swim to Jesus.

___16. Cooked breakfast.

A. Jesus

B. The women in Mark's Gospel

C. Cleopas

D. The guards

E. Peter

F. John

G. The women in Luke's Gospel

H. Mary of Magdala (Magdalene)

I. Thomas

J. The chief priests and elders

K. Andrew

L. An angel

M. The apostles

The Holy Spirit

Catechism paragraphs 535–537, 731–747

In Lesson 7 you learned that Jesus promised to send the Holy Spirit after his ascension. The Gospel of John reports that Jesus made this promise at the Last Supper, saying:

> I still have many things to say to you, but you cannot bear them now. When the Spirit of truth comes, he will guide you into all the truth; for he will not speak on his own but will speak whatever he hears, and he will declare to you the things that are to come. John 16:12-13

On **Pentecost Sunday,** 50 days after Easter, Jesus kept his promise:

> When the day of Pentecost had come, they were all together in one place. And suddenly from heaven there came a sound like the rush of a violent wind, and it filled the entire house where they were sitting. Divided tongues, as of fire, appeared among them, and a tongue rested on each of them. All of them were filled with the Holy Spirit and began to speak in other languages, as the Spirit gave them ability. Acts 2:1-4

It might have been enough if Jesus had just saved us, but he did much more than that. He saved us, but then he stayed on with us and in us. He sent us his Spirit so we could be filled with grace, filled with life, filled with love.

The rest of the **New Testament** is story after story of evidence that the Holy Spirit was alive, teaching and inspiring and filling those early Christians with his gifts. The adventures reported in the Acts of the Apostles, the trials and tribulations Paul reports in his letters, the sermons preached and the advice written, even the very strange dreams John reports in the Book of Revelation—all these are evidence of the Holy Spirit among those early Christians.

What evidence is there today that the Holy Spirit is still alive within the Church?

Know Our Catholic Tradition

Pentecost Sunday is called the "birthday of the Church." This is not just because of the astonishing event about which you just read. The Church's birth was not just a one-day event. What we clearly can see by reading the chapters that follow that story is that the Holy Spirit never stopped moving through the lives of the early Christians from that day on!

You're the Reporter

Choose any two of the six passages from the Acts of the Apostles listed below. For each one, write an attention-getting headline and a good opening paragraph.

Acts 3:1-10   **Acts 5:12-16**   **Acts 7:51-60**

Acts 9:1-9   **Acts 16:25-34**   **Acts 27:6-44**

The Holy Spirit Today

Catechism paragraphs 737–747, 1831–1832, 1835

The Apostles' Creed is the Church's oldest creed. It comes to us from the earliest Church. Look at what early Christians said about the Holy Spirit here: "I believe in the Holy Spirit, the holy **catholic** Church, the **communion of saints,** the forgiveness of sins, the resurrection of the body, and the life everlasting." This statement of our belief in the Holy Spirit is not just the first six words of that sentence, *it is the whole sentence.*

What evidence do we have of the Holy Spirit in the Church today? When the early Christians asked that, here's the evidence they would have pointed to: In spite of a lot of opposition and hardship, we have a Church that makes it possible for us to be holy and that welcomes everyone (that is, a Church that is catholic). We have saints who have gone before us into heaven. Our sins are forgiven. Thanks to Jesus' resurrection we're going to rise someday, too, and we're going to live forever!

There are people who claim that the Holy Spirit isn't very active in the Church today. They claim to look for evidence of the Spirit and find very little or none. Do you think that's true? Have you seen any evidence of the Holy Spirit?

This was a question that concerned St. Paul. In the Letter to the Galatians, he provides a list of what he calls the "fruit of the Spirit," so his readers can check around for evidence of the Holy Spirit's presence. This is what Paul says we'll find: "…the fruit of the Spirit is love, joy, peace, patience, kindness, generosity, faithfulness, gentleness, and self-control" (Galatians 5:22-23). To this list of fruits from St. Paul, the Church has added three more: **modesty,** goodness, and **chastity.**

When we see these **virtues,** we'll know the Holy Spirit is within the person living them. We'll know the Holy Spirit is present in whole families and parishes and schools and communities when we see whole groups of people living them!

Know Our Catholic Tradition

You may also remember the "evidence list" of the work of the Holy Spirit provided as part of Church tradition. We call them the gifts of the Holy Spirit—**wisdom, understanding, counsel, knowledge, fortitude, piety,** and **fear of the Lord.**

You Find the Evidence

What is the evidence that the Holy Spirit is among us now? For each category below, fill in one piece of evidence for each letter in the words "Holy Spirit." For example, for an act of love, you could write, "**H**elped feed the hungry," "**O**rganized a street clean-up," etc.

H O L Y S P I R I T

Acts of courage I have seen or read about:_____

_____

_____

_____

_____

Wise people and the things they do: _____

_____

_____

_____

_____

Acts of love and generosity I've seen or read about: _____

_____

_____

_____

Things I've done because the Holy Spirit is in me: _____

_____

_____

_____

_____

Church Leaders

Catechism paragraphs 874–896, 934–939

We can trace the Catholic Church all the way back to Jesus Christ, who instituted the Church and founded it on the apostles. The leaders of the Church today get their authority from the apostles; they are the direct successors of the apostles.

The Church is a divine institution, founded by the Son of God, and a human institution, existing on earth. For this reason, we need human leadership. We call the leadership of the Church its **hierarchy.** Jesus chose Peter to be the visible head of the Church on earth (Matthew 16:18). With the other apostles, Peter was given authority to rule and guide the Church of Christ.

The successor of Peter in the Church is the pope, the **bishop** of the Church of Rome. The pope has his power from Jesus Christ, just as Peter did. The *Catechism* states this about the pope's authority: "The pope enjoys, by divine institution, supreme, full, immediate, and universal power in the care of souls" (paragraph 937). Just as Peter had the other apostles to serve and rule the Church with him, so the pope has a group of leaders to rule in union with him: the college of bishops. The bishops from every **diocese** in the world make up this body of bishops. At times, the pope will gather this whole college of bishops to discuss and decide with him matters having to do with the life of the Church. Such a gathering is called an **ecumenical council**.

Some bishops are raised to higher honors while still being bishops. **Archbishops** lead very large dioceses called **archdioceses.** Bishops who are raised to the office of **cardinal** are honored in a special way for their service to the Church. The college of cardinals is the group that gathers in Rome to elect a new pope whenever one dies, retires, or resigns.

All bishops have the responsibility to teach the faith, to help people grow in holiness, and to guide the Church. In order to carry out these responsibilities, bishops ordain **priests** to be their co-workers.

When a priest is ordained, he promises **obedience** to the bishop who is ordaining him. He promises to serve the diocese in whatever way he is needed by the bishop. Bishops give priests responsibilities as pastors, teachers, preachers, confessors, and in all ways needed to carry out the mission of the Church for the people in that diocese.

Also ordained to work with the bishop are deacons. All priests are first ordained deacons and usually remain deacons for about a year. There is another group of permanent deacons who remain deacons for the rest of their lives. All deacons **vow** to serve the bishop who ordains them. They are called to works of charity and some liturgical duties, such as preaching, baptizing, and presiding at weddings.

Know Our Catholic Belief

When the pope, in union with the bishops, teaches officially on a matter of revelation, doctrine, or morals, and when this teaching is meant to be believed by the whole Church, he is **infallible;** he speaks without error, guided by the Holy Spirit.

Clues and Transfers

Refer to Lesson 10 for clues to the following statements. When a line has a number beneath it, transfer that letter to the blank marked with that number at the bottom of the page. When you are finished, the transfers will spell an important message.

1. __ __ __ __ __ __   __ __ __ __ __ __ himself instituted the Church.
        6 17   4 7 11

2. The human leadership of the Church is called its __ __ __ __ __ __ __ __ __ .
                                                      28 5   9   22

3. The successor of __ __ __ __ __ is the pope. When speaking officially of
                           26

    Church doctrine he is __ __ __ __ __ __ __ __ __ __ .
                          14 19   16

4. A gathering of bishops with the pope for discussion and decisions about the

    Church is called an __ __ __ __ __ __ __ __ __ __ council.
                        25 21   15

5. The __ __ __ __ __ __ __ of cardinals gathers to elect a new __ __ __ __ .
        23 8   1

6. Bishops ordain __ __ __ __ __ __ __ to be their __ __ —
                   13   3

    __ __ __ __ __ __ __ in a diocese.
    12   10

7. __ __ __ __ __ __ __ are called to do works of __ __ __ __ __ __ __ and to
    20   27   2   24   18

    liturgical duties.

THE MESSAGE:

__ __ __ __ __ __ __ __ __ __ __ __ __ __ __ __ __ __ __
1 2   3 4 5 6   7 8 9 10 11 12 13 14 15 16 17 18 19 20

__ __ __ __ __ __ __ __ .
21 22 23 24 25 26 27 28

The Lay Faithful

Catechism paragraphs 897–913, 940–943

In the Church, baptized people who are not ordained or are not members of a religious community are called the **laity,** or *lay people.* At Baptism, every person is called to share in three missions with Jesus Christ. We are called to be *priests, prophets, and kings.* What can this mean for the many lay men and lay women in the Church? What can this mean for the Church?

The laity share in the *priesthood* of Christ because they are called to help bring the kingdom of God into the world. When baptized lay persons live their faith, they bring grace to their personal, family, and social lives, not just to their lives in the Church. They live their lives in Christ every minute and in every place, and in this way help to make the world holy.

The laity share in the *prophetic* role of Christ in the same way. They are called by their Baptism to be witnesses to Christ—all the time, in all parts of their lives. Their lives and their words tell others about Jesus. The laity are called to **evangelize,** that is, to tell others about the Good News of Christ and to invite them to join the Church or to renew their commitment to the Church.

The laity share in Christ's *kingly* office, too. The kingship of Christ was not exercised on a royal throne but on the cross. His kingship conquered sin and death. The laity, therefore, share in Christ's kingship by overcoming sin in their own lives and by working to remove evils that tempt people to sin.

While living their baptismal call in their everyday lives, the laity bring Christ to their homes, work places, neighborhoods, governments, and places of recreation. Lay people also are often called to serve within their Church communities. They may serve as lay ministers who cooperate with their pastors in the service of their parish community.

Know Our Catholic Tradition

Pope Pius XII once said, "Lay believers are in the front line of Church life" (*Catechism,* paragraph 899).

Three Missions

Write all the letters under a "1" on the line in the box marked "priest" below. Write all the letters under a "2" on the line in the box marked "prophet", and those under a "3" on the line in the box marked "king." Keep the letters in order, and you will spell out one way the lay faithful in the Church live out this mission in Christ's life.

3	1	2	3	1	3	2	1	1	3	2	1	3
O	D	T	V	O	E	E	J	U	R	L	S	C

2	3	1	1	2	3	3	1	2	1	3	2	1
L	O	T	I	O	M	E	C	T	E	S	H	I

1	1	2	3	1	3	2	2	1	3	1	2	2
N	W	E	I	O	N	R	S	R	I	K	A	B

2	1	3	1	3	3	1	2	1	3	2	3	2
O	P	N	L	O	N	A	U	C	E	T	S	F

3	2	3	3	2	2	3	2	1
L	A	I	F	I	T	E	H	E

PRIEST

_____

_____

PROPHET

_____

_____

KING

_____

_____

Catechism paragraphs 914–933, 944–945

In the Gospels, Jesus tells every Christian how to live. The Church has identified from his many teachings three **evangelical counsels** that we are all to put into practice in whatever state of life we live.

These evangelical counsels are: **poverty,** chastity, and obedience. We live poverty not by being destitute but by being "poor in spirit," by not putting material possessions ahead of God and the good of other people. We live chastity by being pure in body, mind, and soul. We live obedience by listening to and following the will of those with legitimate authority over us.

Some people choose to live the evangelical counsels in a life consecrated to God. There is no separate sacrament given to people who wish to live a consecrated life. For them, the sacrament of Baptism is the source of their consecration. They choose to make public vows—solemn promises— binding them to God and the Church by the evangelical counsels.

There are many forms of consecrated life. Most familiar to us is *vowed religious life.* The men who make religious vows might be ordained priests. If not, they are religious brothers. The women who make vows are religious sisters. Vowed religious usually belong to a religious community.

Each community is a group of sisters, or of priests and brothers, who follow a rule approved by the Church, which sets out how they will live their vows together and how they will serve God and the Church.

Men and women who make a vow of poverty promise to own nothing of their own. Members of a religious community own everything in common. They share all their incomes and belongings with everyone else in the community, and they use their possessions for the service of God and the Church.

Those who make a vow of chastity promise never to marry and to give up all sexual intimacy. In this way, vowed religious men and women can dedicate their hearts completely to God and their lives completely to his service.

Those who make a vow of obedience put their own personal wills second to the will of God expressed through the Church, the authorities of their religious community, and the other members of the community. They go where they are told they are needed, and they do the work they are asked to do. Their dedication to God and the Church makes it possible for them to obey those in authority with generous love.

Know Our Catholic Tradition

Three of the most famous saints who founded religious orders are St. Benedict, who is now followed by Benedictine priests, brothers, and sisters all over the world; St. Francis of Assisi, with his Franciscan brothers and sisters still among us today; and St. Dominic, whose Dominican followers still preach and teach worldwide.

The Evangelical Counsels

Look over the descriptions of the three evangelical counsels in Lesson 12. As you read each story below, decide which evangelical counsel—poverty, chastity, or obedience—is being lived or is needed in each case and write it on the line.

When Sue was setting up her own shop in a new town, she learned there were limits on the size and colors she could use for her store's sign.

Which evangelical counsel? _____

Whenever Ben earns any money mowing lawns, he tithes the first ten percent of his earnings by giving it to the soup kitchen his parish sponsors.

Which evangelical counsel? _____

Fr. William has been the pastor at St. James Parish for ten years. This morning he got a letter from the abbot of his religious order assigning him to leave St. James and go to work in the missions in Central America.

Which evangelical counsel? _____

You decide to stay home when you find out the boy-girl party at your friend's house is going to take place when his parents are out of town.

Which evangelical counsel? _____

Fred doesn't see why his parents have to monitor his use of the Internet, but they told him there are too many pornographic materials available, and they want to help him avoid them.

Which *two* evangelical counsels?

_____

_____

When Beth goes to Allison's house, she and Allison have a lot of fun with Allison's computer games and her stuffed toy collection. When they are at Beth's house, however, Beth says, "No one touches my stuff but me."

Which evangelical counsel? _____

Mary, Mother of God

Catechism paragraphs 487–511, 963–975

The Son of God needed a human mother to become a human being. The Incarnation would have been impossible without Mary.

Mary didn't just become the mother of Jesus' human body. She became Jesus' mother, and Jesus is true God and true man. So Mary is the mother of Jesus, God and man. The Church honors her with the title **Theotokos,** which means "Mother of God."

The Church also recognizes that in order for Mary to be the mother of God, who is without sin, she herself would also need to be without sin. The doctrine of the **Immaculate Conception** says that from the moment she was conceived in her mother's womb, Mary was free from **original sin.** We celebrate the Feast of the Immaculate Conception on December 8.

When the angel Gabriel came to her to announce that God wanted her to be the mother of his Son, she did not understand how this could be. She nevertheless agreed to God's request (see Luke 1:38). We celebrate the Feast of the Annunciation on March 25.

Jesus did not have a human father. Mary conceived Jesus through the power of the Holy Spirit. She was a virgin when she conceived Jesus, and she remained a virgin, never physically intimate with any man, throughout her life.

Mary is part of the communion of saints, and with the saints in heaven, she is our model and our intercessor. Mary, however, is more than our model; she is our mother. We give her the title Mother of the Church because as he was dying on the cross, Jesus gave Mary to John and through him to all of us (John 19:26-27).

Because she was always free from sin, God took both her **soul** and her body into heaven at her death. This is the doctrine of the **Assumption.** God has honored his mother in this special way because of her goodness and faith. Now she lives in heaven where she watches over us as Queen of Heaven and a loving mother. We celebrate the Feast of the Assumption on August 15.

Know Our Catholic Belief

Mary is not God, and we do not pray to her as if she is God.
The Church calls her a mediator of grace.
This means we pray to Mary to ask her to speak to God for us.

You're the Editor

A reporter who has very little knowledge of the Church was sent to interview a group of Catholics about their beliefs in Mary. Here is part of her news story. Does she have all the facts straight? The article is double-spaced so you can do some editing. Cross out any incorrect facts and write your corrections above them. Can you find fifteen mistakes?

Catholics have many beliefs about Mary, the mother of Jesus. She is called

"Theotokos" because she is the mother of the human part of Jesus. On December

25, the Church celebrates the Feast of the Immaculate Conception, which says

Jesus was conceived without original sin. On March 25, they celebrate the feast of

the Assumption, the day the angel Michael came to Mary and told her she had to

be the mother of Jesus. Mary was a virgin before she had Jesus, but not after he

was born. Catholics call Mary the Mother of the Church because John gave Mary

to Peter right after Jesus died on the cross. Mary wasn't there when Jesus died.

Catholics also call her the Queen of Heaven because of the doctrine of the

Annunciation. This doctrine says God has taken Mary's soul to heaven and will

take her body to heaven someday, too. This is why Catholics say she is God and

pray to her just like they do to God. They believe Mary can give them grace.

Catechism paragraphs 988–1060

Each human being is made up of both a material body and a spiritual soul. Our bodies will die, but our souls will never die. At our deaths our souls will be separated from our bodies. At the moment of death, each soul will experience a **particular judgment,** a review of how we have lived our lives in Christ and how we have shown our love. The souls that are free from sin and purified through **penance** from all past sins will go to be with God in heaven.

Souls that are not free and purified from all sin will not yet enter heaven but will go through a time of purification and suffering separated from God called **purgatory.** They need our prayers asking God to bring them into heaven.

The saints in heaven are already living eternal life. The souls in purgatory and we on earth hope to one day do the same. There are souls, however, who have no hope of eternal life. They are in a state of eternal death called **hell.**

Although God wants all of us with him in heaven, he gave us all **free will.** If we choose to turn away from him by committing **mortal sin** and refusing to repent, we have chosen to stay separated from him for all eternity. This state of eternal separation is torture because we were created to be with God and will never be perfectly happy without him.

The phrase "resurrection of the body" refers to the belief that, at the end of time, our bodies will rise again and be reunited with our souls. On that last day we will all be judged again in the Last Judgment. At that time, each of us—body and soul—will stand before the throne of Christ and be judged for all we have done and failed to do.

At the end of time, we believe the kingdom of God will come in its fullness. Christ will reign forever in his glorified body and soul. Those with him in heaven will rule with him body and soul, and the material world will be transformed.

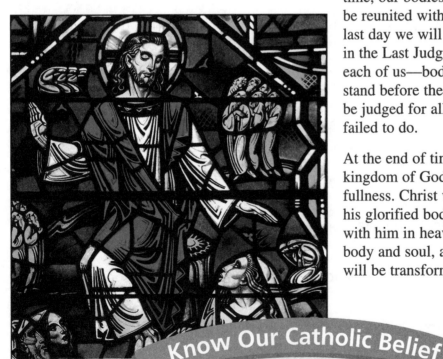

Know Our Catholic Belief

St. Paul says that at the end of time, God will be "all in all" (1 Corinthians 15:28).

Word Search

Use Lesson 14 to answer the questions below and search for them in the puzzle grid. When you have circled all the words, the remaining letters, written in order, will spell a hidden message.

```
G   L   O   K   R   C   H   R   I   S   T
P   A   R   T   I   C   U   L   A   R   D
W   U   E   D   S   N   O   I   A   B   L
R   T   I   E   E   V   G   N   O   S   L
E   I   G   I   E   B   S   D   T   M   C
U   R   N   F   E   F   Y   N   O   H   A
N   I   L   I   O   L   I   R   O   M   E
I   P   U   R   G   A   T   O   R   Y   P
T   S   M   U   S   A   S   S   A   I   O
E   E   N   P   L   E   A   R   A   L   H
D   E   A   T   H   A   P   P   Y   L   L
```

1. We each have a material _____.
2. Because God gave us free will, we can _____ to turn away from him.
3. At the end of life, _____ will judge us.
4. Hell is a place of eternal _____.
5. We cannot be perfectly _____ without God.
6. Souls in hell have no _____ of eternal life.
7. The _____ of God will come in its fullness at the end of time.
8. At the end of time, we will be judged again at the _____ Judgment.
9. We shall be judged by how we live our lives in Christ, by how we show our _____.
10. _____ sin separates us from God.
11. We will have an individual or _____ judgment at the moment of death.
12. We should remember to _____ for the souls in purgatory.
13. _____ is a time of purification and suffering to make up for sins.
14. Before we can enter heaven, our souls must be _____.
15. Christ will _____ forever in his glorified body and soul.
16. At the end of time, our bodies will be _____ with our souls.
17. At the end of time, our bodies will _____ again.
18. Souls in heaven are called _____.
19. We each have a _____ soul.
20. At the end of time, the material world will be _____.

HIDDEN MESSAGE:

_____ .

Review

Mark a "T" in front of any statement that is true. Mark an "F" in front of false statements, and then CHANGE THE STATEMENT TO MAKE IT TRUE.

____ 1. There will continue to be new revelations of God.

____ 2. God remains a mystery beyond words, so it is wrong to talk about him.

____ 3. It is central to our Catholic faith that we believe there is only one God and three persons in one God.

____ 4. Each person in the Trinity works separately on his different missions.

____ 5. The authors of the books of the Bible were inspired by God to write religious truths.

____ 6. In the Incarnation, Jesus became like us in everything, even sin.

____ 7. Pentecost Sunday is called the "birthday of the Church."

Circle the best answer for each question below.

1. The Holy Spirit sanctifies us _____.
   a. when we read the Bible   b. by filling our souls with grace
   c. when we ask

2. Jesus Christ is the _____ between God and all of humanity.
   a. mediator   b. brother   c. Messiah

3. The Incarnation really means _____.
   a. Christmas is a holy day
   b. Jesus became human for each one of us   c. Jesus' death

4. For Christians the cross is _____.
   a. an instrument of torture   b. an instrument of devotion
   c. an instrument of salvation

5. The Holy Spirit _____.
   a. is active in the lives of people of faith today
   b. isn't as active as he used to be   c. is Jesus

6. The lay faithful in the Church share in Christ's priesthood by _____.
   a. saying Mass   b. bringing Christ into their daily world
   c. working at Church

7. The doctrine of the _____ teaches Mary is in heaven, body, and soul.
   a. Immaculate Conception   b. Assumption   c. Incarnation

Section Two
Our Catholic Celebrations

The second part of the *Catechism* is titled "The Celebration of the Christian Mystery." This part teaches us about our liturgical celebrations of the seven sacraments.

Perhaps you have become more involved in liturgical celebrations in your parish. Or perhaps you have drawn away from them recently. Either way, use this section to review why and how we celebrate the Mass and the sacraments and to expand your appreciation and knowledge of the liturgy. You are now at an age where you can understand more and enter more fully into the Church's celebrations. Doing this could really help renew your life in Christ.

Catechism paragraphs 1066–1187

God's plan of salvation is not just about doctrines of faith, lists of things to know we believe. God's plan is about *persons.* God the Father, God the Son (Jesus), and God the Holy Spirit are all alive and acting in our lives now. Mary is with God in heaven interceding for us. The angels and saints are in heaven, too. Even the souls waiting in purgatory are living souls. All these persons are part of our salvation. Then there are all the persons on earth— starting with ourselves and reaching out to all our neighbors. Since God's plan of salvation is about so much more than listing what we believe, what do we *do* about it?

Here is the Church's answer to that question: We "do" **liturgy.** Liturgy is the way we celebrate *what we believe.* The *Catechism* calls liturgy "the participation of the People of God in the work of God" (paragraph 1069). Now, we already know the "work of God." It is our *salvation and sanctification.* This is why God became human and why the human Jesus sent us his Holy Spirit. In the Church, it is our turn to participate.

Here on earth, through the **sacraments,** we already have a foretaste of heaven. We could never imagine this on our own, but God has revealed it to us through Jesus Christ. Our liturgical celebrations—the Mass, the sacraments, our other liturgical devotions—give us grace, make us holy, save us, and unite us with God.

In liturgical gatherings, especially the Eucharistic Liturgy (the Mass), we meet Jesus Christ in the Word of Scripture and in the Eucharist. We are offered forgiveness of sins. We are given God's life (grace).

Know Our Catholic Belief

The next time you go to Mass, listen carefully to the words of the eucharistic prayer. All of us will hear words and phrases that point to our participation in God's work of saving us and to all those persons involved with us. If you find yourself saying, "But those are just words," or if you wonder, "What do those words have to do with me?" read on! Remember, Jesus became human and lived and died and rose from the dead *for you.* The Mass isn't just about "our salvation"; it is about *your* salvation!

Meditation on a Eucharistic Prayer

The italicized lines below are from Eucharistic Prayer III. Use the sentence starters under each line to write some personal thoughts about what these words say to you.

Father,… all life, all holiness comes from you through Jesus Christ our Lord, by the working of the Holy Spirit.

God, I am especially grateful for the life I see in _____

_____

_____.

I have also seen holiness around me, and I know it comes from you. The holiness

I'm grateful for is _____

_____.

From age to age you gather a people to yourself…

God, these words tell me _____

_____.

Take this, all of you, and eat it: This is my body which will be given up for you.

God, when the priest says these words at Mass, I _____

_____.

…ready to greet [Christ] when he comes again…

Jesus, am I ready to greet you when you come again at my own judgment or the

Last Judgment? The ways I think I am ready are _____

_____.

The ways I fear I might not be ready and need your help are _____

_____.

May [Christ] make us an everlasting gift to you…

God, can we human beings really be a gift you want? Here is how I know

I am a gift: _____

_____.

Catechism paragraphs 1135–1199

How much do you feel at home in your church building? Have you been a member of your parish a long or short while? Do you know who is leading your parish celebrations? What items are they using? Where in the church building are they doing the celebrations? What do their actions and the symbols around you mean? What are you supposed to do and say?

Have you ever wondered how Catholics in other parts of the world celebrate the liturgy? How are we alike, and how are we different? Some of these questions are discussed in other parts of this book, especially in this second section. In this lesson, let's focus on the tangible, visible objects and actions you see and hear all around you.

Many objects used for liturgy are beautiful, but they are meant to be more than decoration. Look around your parish church. Where is the **altar,** the table on which the Eucharist is celebrated? The altar is made either of stone or wood with a stone set in it. Relics of saints are sealed into this stone as a sign of our communion with the saints. The priest places the Body of Christ on the altar at that spot, and he kisses the altar where the Eucharist will lie as a sign of reverence.

Now locate the tabernacle, the place where the Blessed Sacrament is kept. It might be near the altar or in another place of honor. A **sanctuary lamp** is kept burning there at all times as a reminder of Christ's presence. His presence is also the reason we **genuflect** on one knee when we walk in front of the tabernacle.

Do you also see a cabinet where the holy oils are kept? Sacred **chrism** is kept there, and often the **oil of catechumens** and the oil of the sick are there, too.

You might think you can't find the **ambo,** but you will recognize it by its other name—the lectern. From this holy place, the Word of God is proclaimed. The **celebrant,** deacon, and **lectors** use a book called the **lectionary** to read selections from Scripture.

Where is your parish **baptistry?** It is here that your parish gathers to baptize new members into the Church. That font and any holy water fonts also remind us of our own Baptisms. Be sure to use the holy water to sign yourself with the Sign of the Cross as you thank God for your gift of faith.

Know Our Catholic Belief

Catholics are part of a sacramental Church, so we believe we can meet God through our senses. We believe our physical selves need help to get in touch with spiritual truths. This is why we place flowers and art—stained glass windows, statues, paintings, banners—all around us. Even our church architecture is meant to express something about our faith. We also sing and have music as part of our celebrations. These help us raise our minds and hearts to God.

Clues and Transfers

Refer to Lesson 16 to fill in each blank below. When a line has a number beneath it, transfer that letter to the blank marked with that number at the bottom of the page. When you are finished, the transfers will spell an important message.

1. The Catholic Church is a __ __ __ __ __ __ __ __ __ __ __ Church.
                             28   15   6 2 25 9

2. We __ __ __ __ to help us raise our __ __ __ __ __ and hearts to __ __ __.
         5 10   12   18 20

3. We __ __ __ __ __ __ __ __ __ on one knee in front
         7   21   27   13

   of the __ __ __ __ __ __ __ __ __ __ where a __ __ __ __ __ __ __ __ __
               8 22   24   23   3   17

   lamp burns at all times as a reminder of Christ's presence.

4. The __ __ __ __   __ __ __ __ used for anointing in several sacraments
       19 11   16   26

   are kept in a special cabinet.

5. We keep __ __ __ __   __ __ __ __ __ in fonts to remind us of Baptism.
         14   1 4

THE MESSAGE:

__ __   __ __ __   __ __ __ __   __ __ __   __ __ __ __ __ __ __
1 2   3 4 5   6 7 8 9   10 11 12   13 14 15 16 17 18 19

__ __ __   __ __ __ __ __ __.
20 21 22   23 24 25 26 27 28

Catechism paragraphs 1200–1209

We know the Church is **one,** holy, catholic, and **apostolic.** We can find these marks of the Church in any Catholic Church we visit anywhere in the world. Yet, this does not mean we are identical all over the world!

The liturgy is one, but the forms of liturgical celebration are different from one century to the next, one country to the next, and one culture to the next. Because the Church is a missionary Church that reaches out with the message of Christ to people of all lands, it stands to reason that some forms of celebration would be different. As long as the truths being taught and celebrated are faithful to the teachings of the Catholic Church, different forms of liturgical celebration are still legitimate.

If a Church celebrates a Eucharistic Liturgy that does not proclaim that the bread and wine of the Eucharist actually become the Body and Blood of Christ, that religious denomination is Christian, but it is not Catholic. There are several groups of Catholics who teach that the Eucharist is truly the Body and Blood of Christ. The Church then asks these groups if they are also obedient to the pope, the head of the Church in Rome. Groups of Catholics who acknowledge the authority of the pope but who celebrate the liturgy differently from the Roman Church are referred to as Churches of a *different rite.*

The liturgies of these different rites contain many prayers and actions that are the same. The seven sacraments are all celebrated. Bread and wine are **consecrated** and become the Body and Blood of Christ. Some of the prayers prayed and symbols used, however, will be different and some of the regulations for the reception of sacraments will differ, too.

No wonder the Church is called catholic! The word means "universal," and we can see how far the Church reaches to embrace people of all times and places.

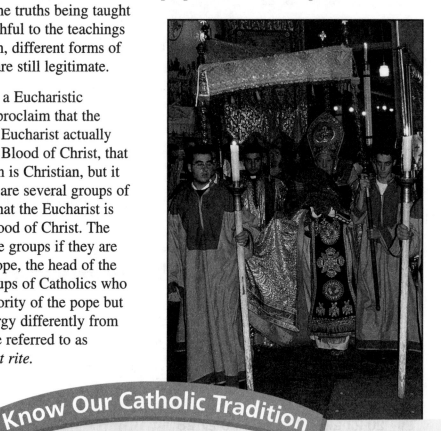

Know Our Catholic Tradition

You and your family might be members of a different Catholic rite. Here in the United States, most Catholics use the Latin, or Roman, rite. Smaller groups of Catholics belong to one of the **Eastern rites:** the Byzantine, Coptic, Syriac, Armenian, Maronite, or Chaldean rites.

Crossword Puzzle

Solve the crossword puzzle using what you have learned in Lesson 17.

ACROSS

2. The Catholic Church celebrates _____ sacraments.
4. To be Catholic, a group must be obedient to the _____ in Rome.
5. The Church is a _____ Church who reaches out to all lands.
6. Whether Catholic or not, if a Church follows Christ, it is _____.
8. In the U.S. most Catholics use the _____, or Roman, rite.
9. When we say the Church is one, we are speaking of one of the four _____ of the Church.
11. Religious denominations that do not believe the _____ is actually the Body and Blood of Christ are not Catholic.
12. Groups faithful to the pope but celebrating liturgy differently belong to a different _____.

DOWN

1. Forms of liturgical _____ can differ from place to place.
3. Different forms of liturgy are _____ as long as things taught are faithful to Church teaching.
7. Smaller groups of Catholics belong to an _____ rite such as the Byzantine rite.
10. Universal means _____.

Catechism paragraphs 1213–1284

Take a moment to think about how it feels to splash water on your face during a hot day or about the last time you went swimming. Can you remember the refreshment you felt?

The Church goes to a lot of trouble to get us to think of water, in this case, the waters of Baptism. The "big night" for initiation into the Church is Holy Saturday night. All three **sacraments of initiation** are celebrated, and just before the celebration we hear some Old Testament stories about water. First we hear the story from Genesis in which God creates water and all life. Then we hear Exodus 14:15—15:1 in which God saves the Israelites by letting them cross through the sea as if it were dry land.

Do you remember how the Paschal candle is plunged into the water that night? It is a symbol of Christ's death and burial. The Church puts a double message before us: Water refreshes and gives life, and water drowns and destroys.

So what does this double message have to do with Baptism? Some parishes baptize older children or adults by **immersion** and totally lower the person under water. It's a little harder to understand the message of Baptism when water is simply poured on the head, but the Church still wants us to understand the message: *In Baptism you die and are buried. You die to your old self and to sin. In Baptism you are refreshed; you are washed clean. You rise from the water newly alive. In Baptism you are saved.*

At your Baptism, you were also anointed with two kinds of oil: the oil of catechumens for protection from evil and chrism to keep you strong in Christ's priesthood. You were given a candle and told to carry the light of Christ. You received a white garment as a sign of your spotless soul and were told to keep it that way. Do you ever feel some regret over losing that sinless innocence you had on your Baptism day? Remember this: Your Baptism wasn't just a one-day event. True, it leaves a permanent **character** on your soul and can be received only once, but it still wasn't just a one-day event.

The effects of your Baptism go on forever. Even if you break your friendship with God, because of your Baptism you can come to the Church for forgiveness. Because of Baptism, you can be fed with the Eucharist; you can receive the gift of the Spirit; you can be anointed if you are sick. The grace of your Baptism is always available for you.

Know Our Catholic Belief

The Church teaches that Baptism is necessary to be saved. Because God is a loving Father, we trust in his mercy to save infants and children who die without Baptism. Others who die without Baptism can also be saved through the grace of Christ if they die to defend the faith, if they are preparing for Baptism, or if they, without knowing of the Church, still seek God sincerely and strive to do his will.

Liturgical Designs

Your parish has decided to change the decorations of the articles used for the Baptism of infants and small children. Decorate the baptismal candle, the white garment, the baptismal font, and a banner to hang in front of the ambo. Be sure your decorations include symbols that represent the various themes and messages of Baptism mentioned in Lesson 18.

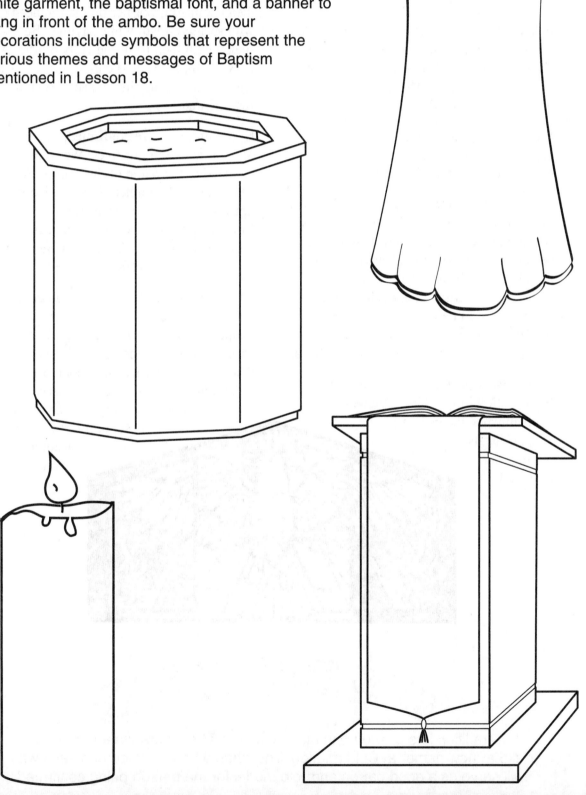

Catechism paragraphs 1285–1321

Baptism and **Confirmation** are closely linked. In the Latin rite, older children and adults are confirmed and baptized in the **Rite of Christian Initiation of Adults** on Holy Saturday night. The grace of Baptism is not complete until we are confirmed.

Like Baptism, Confirmation imprints a permanent spiritual character on the soul, so a person can only be confirmed once.

Unless the person to be confirmed is an infant or very young child, the Church has some requirements for Confirmation: The person must be baptized, profess his or her faith in Christ, be in a state of grace, and really want Confirmation. Each person confirmed must be willing to be an active member of the Church who gives witness to a belief in Christ by the way he or she lives.

Confirmation usually takes place during a Eucharistic Liturgy. The sacrament is given when the bishop lays his hands on the person's head and

then anoints him or her on the forehead with sacred chrism while saying, "Be sealed with the gift of the Holy Spirit." As in Baptism, the sacred chrism is used as a sign of our sharing in the priesthood of Jesus Christ.

Even before we are confirmed, the Holy Spirit is active in our lives. We were baptized in the name of the Trinity, and have had God—Father, Son, and Holy Spirit—with us ever since. With Confirmation, we receive an increase in the gifts of the Holy Spirit. Our Baptism is "sealed," made official, ratified.

Each person is confirmed with a **sponsor** at his or her side. Some people choose a godparent to return and serve as sponsor. Others choose another Catholic person who would be a good role model for Christian living. The sponsor serves as a witness and as a sign of the support of the whole Church community.

Know Our Catholic Tradition

A tradition has grown up in many places that encourages a person to take a "new name" at Confirmation. This should be the name of a saint who will serve as a good patron and role model for the person being confirmed.

Role Descriptions

When it is time, a young person has some decisions to make about Confirmation: Am I ready to be confirmed? Whom will I choose for my sponsor? Whom will I choose for my patron saint? Think about your "personal requirements" for each of these roles and write your ideas below:

Am I ready to be confirmed?
List at least six requirements you personally want to meet in order to be confirmed:

1. _____
2. _____
3. _____
4. _____
5. _____
6. _____

Whom will I choose for my sponsor?
List at least six qualities you will look for in a Confirmation sponsor:

1. _____
2. _____
3. _____
4. _____
5. _____
6. _____

Whom will I choose for my patron saint?
List at least six qualities you will look for in a patron saint for Confirmation:

1. _____
2. _____
3. _____
4. _____
5. _____
6. _____

Catechism paragraphs 1136–1144, 1345–1419

No other sacrament is celebrated as often as the Eucharist. The Eucharistic Liturgy, or the Mass, is celebrated in most parish churches and in other Catholic chapels nearly every day! We Catholics are obliged to participate in the Eucharistic Liturgy each Saturday evening or Sunday.

The word "Eucharist" means "thanksgiving," so there is always an emphasis on giving God perfect thanks and praise. We can only do this perfectly because we offer God his own Son.

In the Eucharistic Liturgy bread and wine are consecrated. This consecration brings about a change called **transubstantiation.** The bread is no longer bread. It looks like bread, but it is now the Body of Christ. Likewise, the wine is no longer wine after the consecration. It is now the Blood of Christ.

The priest who presides at Mass is called the celebrant. Only a priest or bishop can consecrate the bread and wine.

Lectors read the Old and New Testament readings during the **Liturgy of the Word.** A **cantor** sings the Responsorial Psalm and leads the congregation in song. A choir or other ministers of music might sing or accompany the singing. All these ministers place their gifts at the service of the Church. Another liturgical role you may have taken is the altar server who brings the priest the things needed at the altar and answers all the prayers of the Mass.

Specially trained lay persons, called **eucharistic ministers**, might help distribute Holy Communion. These people also often take the Eucharist to parishioners who are sick or shut-in.

Unless we have mortal sin on our souls, we are encouraged to receive the Eucharist each time we come to Mass. The Eucharist unites us closely with Jesus, forgives our **venial sins** (less serious sins), gives us grace to avoid sin, and strengthens the unity of all members in the Church.

Know Our Catholic Tradition

Each Eucharistic Liturgy includes:
- the proclamation of the Word of God from Scripture;
- prayers of thanksgiving to God for all his gifts, especially his Son, Jesus;
- the consecration of the bread and wine during the **Liturgy of the Eucharist;**
- and the reception of the Body and Blood of Christ in Holy Communion.

Prayers of Liturgical Ministers

Write prayers that a parish could use for each of the ministers listed below. Be sure that in each prayer you speak specifically about the role that person will play in the Eucharistic Liturgy, what help he or she needs from God, and why it is a privilege to share in the eucharistic celebration this way.

Prayer of the lector:

_____

_____

_____

_____

_____

_____

_____

Prayer of an altar server:

_____

_____

_____

_____

_____

_____

_____

Prayer of the cantor and other ministers of music:

_____

_____

_____

_____

_____

_____

_____

Prayer of the eucharistic ministers:

_____

_____

_____

_____

_____

_____

_____

Eucharistic Devotions

Catechism paragraphs 1377–1381, 1418

Have you seen how carefully the ministers at the altar clean and wipe the **chalice** (the special cup used at Mass) after everyone has received Holy Communion? The celebrant, deacon, or eucharistic ministers usually make sure there is none of Christ's Blood left in the chalice. Every drop and every crumb of the Eucharist must be cleaned up. Even the **corporal,** the cloth laid on the altar upon which the sacrament is placed, and the **purificators,** the smaller strips of cloth used to wipe the chalices, are rinsed separately from the regular church laundry. The water used to rinse the chalice is poured into a special sink in the **sacristy** with a pipe that goes directly into the earth.

Special unleavened breads called **hosts** are consecrated at Mass. The uneaten consecrated hosts remain the Body of Christ. They are placed in a covered cup or dish called a **ciborium,** kept in the tabernacle. Why all this special attention? When the priest consecrates the bread and wine, they become the Body and Blood of Christ, and they remain so after the Eucharistic Liturgy is ended.

A number of special devotions and prayerful practices show our faith in the Eucharist.

One of these is private adoration of the Eucharist. Since Christ is present in the tabernacle, many people like to spend time alone in prayer before the tabernacle, knowing they are praying in the presence of Jesus himself. We also have public adoration of the Eucharist. In this case, the Eucharist is placed outside the tabernacle, often in a **monstrance,** a decorated container with a window in it through which the Eucharist can be seen. During public adoration, the Eucharist is never left alone.

Parishes sometimes have a holy hour during which people gather to pray. Others might have a 40 hours devotion, in which the Eucharist is exposed for 40 hours, and people take turns spending time in adoration around the clock. Some parishes, convents, and monasteries have perpetual adoration.

A public ceremony of adoration is called **Benediction of the Blessed Sacrament.** The Eucharist in the monstrance is adored with songs and prayers and then raised high in blessing. Sometimes the ceremony includes a procession in which the priest or deacon carries the monstrance, leading the faithful in a walk up the aisles of the church.

Know Our Catholic Tradition

We celebrate the institution of the Eucharist on Holy Thursday. Then, in late spring, we have another special Sunday to honor the Eucharist: the Feast of the Body and Blood of Christ. On that day, many parishes have a procession outside into neighborhoods or fields to bless the world with the Eucharist and to ask Christ's protection of our homes, crops, and workplaces.

Word Search

Answer the questions below and search for them in the grid. When you have circled all the words, the remaining letters, written in order, will spell a hidden message.

```
O  E  L  C  A  N  R  E  B  A  T  H
U  S  A  C  R  O  E  Y  Y  N  P  O
P  U  R  I  F  I  C  A  T  O  R  S
E  P  O  B  O  T  N  D  S  I  O  T
R  P  P  O  R  A  A  S  I  T  C  S
P  E  R  R  T  R  R  R  R  C  E  F
E  R  O  I  Y  C  T  U  C  I  S  A
T  A  C  U  I  E  S  H  A  D  S  T
U  T  H  M  I  S  N  T  S  E  I  S
A  L  V  I  S  N  O  I  B  N  O  L
L  A  E  A  N  O  M  D  S  E  N  T
C  H  A  L  I  C  E  R  O  B  N  G
```

1. The _____ is the table on which the bread and wine are consecrated.
2. A _____ is a public ceremony of adoration and blessing.
3. The _____ is the cup used at Mass.
4. The covered dish used to hold the uneaten Eucharist is the _____.
5. The _____ is the blessing that changes bread and wine into Christ's Body and Blood.
6. The cloth on which the Blessed Sacrament is placed is called the _____.
7. A time of adoration around the clock is called _____ hours devotion.
8. _____ are the breads used for the Eucharist.
9. A _____ is the decorated container for viewing the Blessed Sacrament.
10. Some parishes, convents, and monasteries have _____ adoration.
11. A ceremonial walk carrying the Blessed Sacrament is called a _____.
12. A small strip of cloth for wiping the chalice is called a _____.
13. The area behind or to the side of the altar where vestments and vessels are kept is the _____.
14. Jesus instituted the Eucharist at the Last _____.
15. The _____ is the place in Church where the Blessed Sacrament is kept.
16. We celebrate the institution of the Eucharist on Holy _____.

HIDDEN MESSAGE: _____.

Catechism paragraphs 976–987, 1422–1498

Do you remember the first time you received the sacrament of **Penance and Reconciliation?** You might have called it by a different name. Sometimes it is called Penance. Others call it Reconciliation. Either term is correct. An older term, Confession, refers to the action of telling sins to the priest, but it is not the full name of this sacrament.

Penance and Reconciliation is one of two **sacraments of healing.** Jesus often linked the healing of physical illness with the healing of spiritual illness, or sin.

Jesus gave the power to forgive sins to the Church. The Church uses that power in several ways. Besides this sacrament of Penance and Reconciliation:

• Baptism forgives our sins.
• We also can be forgiven in the Eucharist and in
• the sacrament of **Anointing of the Sick.**

So, why should we receive Penance and Reconciliation? We *must* confess mortal sins to a priest and receive **absolution** in the sacrament of Penance and Reconciliation. We are *encouraged* to confess venial sins so we can enjoy the graces of this sacrament. As we get older and need more help overcoming temptation, this sacrament can be a great help.

When we receive this sacrament, the priest gives us a penance to do or say. This is meant to show our sorrow for our sins and to make up in a small way for what we have done. We know, however, that there are more serious consequences to sin for which no simple penance can atone. We will need to be purified before we can go to heaven. Even without mortal sin, unless we live *very* holy lives, we are sure to have some time of suffering ahead of us in purgatory.

Know Our Catholic Belief

We can begin to remove either part or all the punishment for sin by the practice of **indulgences.** We can also help remove the punishment of the souls in purgatory. The Church grants indulgences for certain prayers, devotions, and pious practices.

Penance and Reconciliation Then and Now

Think back to your first celebration of the sacrament of Penance and Reconciliation and make a "Then and Now" comparison chart.

Age when I first celebrated Penance and Reconciliation:

_____

Age I am now:

_____

Typical sins I committed then:

_____

_____

_____

_____

Typical sins I commit now:

_____

_____

_____

_____

What I thought about God then:

_____

_____

_____

What I think about God now:

_____

_____

_____

What made me feel most guilty then:

_____

What makes me feel most guilty now:

_____

What I understood about this sacrament then:

_____

_____

What I understand about this sacrament now:

_____

_____

How I told God I was sorry then:

_____

_____

How I tell God I am sorry now:

_____

_____

Anointing of the Sick

Catechism paragraphs 1499–1532

The second sacrament of healing is for the healing of our souls and bodies. This is the Anointing of the Sick, the sacrament given especially for those who are seriously ill, elderly, or in danger of death.

Illness is part of every person's life. The people of Israel tried to understand the mystery of illness. Why did some people get ill and die while others recovered? Was illness a punishment? They knew they should turn to God during illness. Psalm 41:4 proclaims, "O Lord, be gracious to me; heal me…."

You know the compassion Jesus showed to the sick and disabled. He healed the sick and gave the power of healing to the Church through his apostles. After Pentecost, there are many reports of apostles healing the sick and disabled.

The earliest description of the Church celebrating the sacrament of the Anointing of the Sick comes from the Letter of James, who wrote:

> Are any among you sick? They should call for the elders of the church and have them pray over them, anointing them with oil in the name of the Lord. The prayer of faith will save the sick, and the Lord will raise them up; and anyone who has committed sins will be forgiven. James 5:14-15

Today when we are sick we still "call for the elders," that is, the priests. Only a priest can give the sacrament of the Anointing of the Sick, but other members of the Church are present to pray.

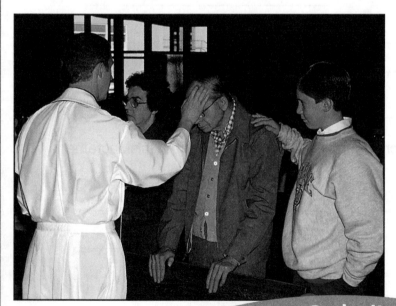

People who are seriously ill and in danger of death should receive this sacrament. So should people with chronic, long-term illnesses and the elderly, even though they are not in immediate danger of death. Anointing gives grace that the sick, disabled, and elderly need to help them in their suffering and unites them to the sufferings of Jesus.

Know Our Catholic Tradition

It is through the touch of human hands that Jesus can touch people with his healing love in the Church today.

Some Sacramental Advice

Here are the letters of three young people close to your age. Each one has a different problem and opinion. How would you answer each one?

Man, am I steamed! Just because I'm going to have surgery on my knee tomorrow, my aunt suggested we call the pastor at church and have him come give me the sacrament of Anointing of the Sick! That's for old and dying people, not for young guys like me! I mean, I'm not going to die or anything. Am I?

Joel

Dear Joel,

_____

_____

_____

_____

_____

Dear Sarah,

_____

_____

_____

_____

_____

My grandma is in a nursing home now, and I haven't gone to see her because I know it'll be too depressing. Next Saturday's her birthday, and my mom says I have to go because we're going to have Mass there. Fr. Joe is going to give her some kind of special sacrament or something. It sounds really boring, so I'm going to try to get out of going.

Sarah

No, I haven't been back to Church since my accident. I'll be in this wheelchair for the rest of my life, so I guess I can't go to Church anymore. I can't get in. What difference does it make anyway? What good has God done for me lately?

Kevin

Dear Kevin,

_____

_____

_____

_____

_____

Catechism paragraphs 1601–1666

The Church has two **sacraments of service: Holy Orders** and **Matrimony.** Holy Orders gives the Church bishops, priests, and deacons. Matrimony gives the Church Christian families.

The sacrament of Matrimony takes the human love of a man and a woman—a love that is already good and of great value—and raises that love to something even higher. Both people vow to love each other *as Christ loves the Church.* This is a much deeper and more perfect love than romantic love! This is a love that will help both the man and the woman become holy. People who marry are to help each other get to heaven.

As soon as a couple makes vows to each other, they become one family, one household. They are to make a home together where Christ is welcome to stay. If God blesses their marriage with children, their home is to be the first place the children will learn about the Catholic faith.

The Church takes the vows of Matrimony very seriously and wants all who marry to take them seriously, too. The Church, therefore, does not allow people to be married to more than one person at a time. It does not allow people to break their vows by turning in love to a person other than their spouse. Matrimony is a sacred bond and covenant, a solemn vow. Part of that vow also includes the willingness to have children. Not all couples are able to conceive children, but couples are not to prevent the conception of children through artificial forms of birth control. They promised on their wedding day to welcome the children God sends them.

Marriage vows are indissoluble. If a couple gets a civil divorce, they are still married in the eyes of the Church, and therefore may not remarry. Divorced people do not separate themselves from the Church and may still receive the Eucharist as long as they do not remarry. Divorced persons who remarry are still members of the Church, but they may not receive the Eucharist. They continue to live Christian lives and are encouraged to continue to raise their children in the Catholic faith.

Married couples are signs of Christ's love not only to each other but to their children, their friends and families, and everyone they meet. The sacrament of Matrimony flows from Baptism. The marriage of two baptized people is a sign of the new covenant of God with his Church.

Know Our Catholic Tradition

Matrimony is always a public celebration, held in the presence of witnesses. A priest or a deacon officiates at the celebration, but *it is the man and woman who give the sacrament of Matrimony to each other.* Husband and wife are the ministers of this sacrament to each other.

Clues and Transfers

Refer to Lesson 24 to fill in each blank below. When a line has a number beneath it, transfer that letter to the blank marked with that number at the bottom of the page. When you are finished, the transfers will spell an important message.

1. Matrimony is always a __ __ __ __ __ __ celebration held in the presence
$\qquad\qquad\qquad$ 13

   of __ __ __ __ __ __ __ __ __.
   $\quad$ 12 $\quad$ 20 4 9

2. The man and the woman __ __ __ __ the sacrament of Matrimony
   $\qquad\qquad\qquad$ 3 $\quad$ 15

   to __ __ __ __ other.
   $\quad$ 16 $\quad$ 8

3. As soon as a couple makes __ __ __ __, they become
   $\qquad\qquad\qquad$ 14

   one __ __ __ __ __ __.
   $\quad$ 6 18 $\quad$ 2

4. A __ __ __ __ __ __ or a __ __ __ __ __ __ officiates at the wedding.
   $\qquad$ 1 7 $\qquad$ 11 $\qquad$ 5 17

5. Matrimony is a sacred bond and __ __ __ __ __ __ __ __.
   $\qquad\qquad\qquad$ 19 $\quad$ 10

THE MESSAGE:

__ __ __ __ __ __ __ __ __ __ __ __ __ __ __ __ __ __ __ __.
1 2 3 4 $\quad$ 5 6 $\quad$ 7 8 9 $\quad$ 10 11 12 $\quad$ 13 14 15 16 17 18 19 20

Sacramentals

Catechism paragraphs 1667–1679

Catholics use material objects and human words to bring us into the presence of the living God. We have studied the seven sacraments and have seen how water, oil, bread, wine, hands, and words can bring us God's salvation. Recall that sacraments are outward signs instituted by Christ so he can give us grace.

You've also noticed that the Church uses many sacred objects to help celebrate the sacraments. The Church also recognizes and uses material things outside the celebration of the sacraments that still bring the sacraments and our salvation to our minds. We call these material things **sacramentals.** Sacramentals are signs instituted by the Church to prepare us to receive the sacraments and to help make us holy.

Sacramentals always include a prayer, usually a Sign of the Cross and, perhaps, holy water. This is important because sometimes people forget that sacramental objects are supposed to prepare us for the sacraments.

Some sacramentals are used all over the world; others are regional. The rosary is an example of a universal sacramental. It has no power of its own, but there is great power in the prayers we pray while using a rosary. The Advent wreath and candles have no power, but they remind us of the liturgical season and help us pray. The Church permits and even encourages regional practices as long as they continue to help people live their lives in Christ.

Blessings of persons, meals, objects, and places are the first form of sacramental. They both praise God for his works and gifts, and offer intercession for those who will use those gifts. We use blessed palms on Palm Sunday and take pieces of it home to remind us of Christ's suffering and death. Extra blessed palms are burned and the ashes blessed and used as a sacramental on Ash Wednesday to help us begin Lent with devotion.

Know Our Catholic Tradition

Everyone can give blessings. We should all bless each meal we eat.
Parents should bless their children, and children can also bless their parents.
If you have an Advent wreath, a Christmas tree, or a manger scene,
your family can bless all these sacramentals.

Write Your Own Blessings

In a blessing, we both *thank* and *praise* God for what he has done through this person or thing we are blessing, and we ask God to take care of and bring blessings upon the person or thing. Using that pattern, write blessings in your own words for the following:

A blessing (or grace) before the meal a family is eating to celebrate the birthday of a grandmother who is 80 years old:

_____

_____

_____

_____

A blessing for one or both of your parents or your guardians:

_____

_____

_____

_____

A blessing for your room:

_____

_____

_____

_____

A blessing for a family gathering on Thanksgiving Day:

_____

_____

_____

_____

Section Two
Review

Mark a "T" in front of any statement that is true. Mark an "F" in front of false statements, and then CHANGE THE STATEMENT TO MAKE IT TRUE.

___ 1. God's plan of salvation is just history; it has nothing to do with us now.

___ 2. If a religion does not believe the bread and wine become the Body and Blood of Christ, it is not part of the Catholic Church.

___ 3. We should only think of water as refreshing and life-giving.

___ 4. Confirmation isn't really that important as long as we are baptized.

___ 5. Eucharistic ministers often take the Eucharist to people who are sick or shut-in.

___ 6. We are encouraged to confess mortal sins in the sacrament of Penance and Reconciliation.

___ 7. The priest gives the sacrament of Matrimony to a man and a woman who get married.

Circle the best answer for each question below.

1. Liturgy is the way we _____.
   a. celebrate what we believe   b. remember our sins
   c. list what we believe

2. We Catholics believe we can meet God through our senses, and so we are _____.
   a. a sacramental Church   b. universal   c. a eucharistic Church

3. When a religious group acknowledges the pope as head of the Church and celebrates liturgy differently from the Roman Church it belongs to a different _____.
   a. denomination   b. century   c. rite

4. The Church teaches that Baptism is _____.
   a. usually for infants   b. necessary to be saved
   c. only for emergencies

5. The word Eucharist means _____.
   a. bread   b. Mass   c. thanksgiving

6. The sacrament of the Anointing of the Sick is _____.
   a. necessary for salvation   b. only for the dying
   c. for anyone who is seriously ill, chronically ill, or elderly

7. Sacramentals are _____.
   a. signs instituted by Christ   b. signs instituted by the Church
   c. not allowed by the Church

Section Three
We Live Our Life in Christ

The third part of the *Catechism* is titled "Life in Christ." As you know well by now, *living* what we believe is a lot harder than just *talking* about it or even singing about it! There are commandments and precepts to follow, but in the end, we are responsible for all the moral decisions we make.

This third section will help you review some basic things you need to know to help you have an informed conscience.

Catechism paragraphs 1701–1715, 1730–1761, 1776–1802

Sometimes you need to decide whether an action you want to do is right or wrong. You have to use your free will responsibly, bringing an informed **conscience** to each **moral decision.** Make any moral decision by first asking the Holy Spirit to guide you as you think through the following steps:

- *What* is being chosen? You need to honestly look at the "object" you are choosing—the action, thing, person— and ask yourself if it is truly good and good for you.

- *Why* is it being chosen? You must have a good intention for what you are choosing, and you must want good to come from your choice. A good intention alone, however, is not enough. The object, as mentioned above, must also be good.

- *What are the circumstances and the consequences of this action?* If they are good, that alone won't make the action good. You need to consider them as you decide what to do. If they are bad, that will be another way you will know the action is wrong.

All three of these sources of morality *must be judged* good for an act to be morally good. To judge, an informed conscience is needed. You can't just decide on your own whether the action or object being chosen is good or evil. Some acts are always wrong, no matter what you want to think of them or what else you hear about them.

You should listen to your conscience if it is warning you about something. At least take time to investigate further. Where do you investigate? How can you find out what Jesus would do and what the Church teaches? You can recall what you have read and heard from Scripture, from homilies, from books, and from classes, and you can turn to a person of faith for wise counsel.

Know Our Catholic Belief

A poorly informed conscience is no excuse for a wrong decision, and a well-formed and informed conscience is a good guide. In fact, once your conscience has made a judgment you are sure is correct, you must follow your conscience.

You Decide!

For each moral decision below, decide where you stand on the issue. Use the guidelines for judging morality from Lesson 26. If you don't have enough information, describe what more you would need to know before you could decide.

1. Sean saw a knife in his friend's pocket. He reported it to the school principal.

   Do you agree with what Sean did? _____

   Strongly disagree   **Sort of disagree**   **Not enough information**   **Sort of agree**   **Strongly agree**

   What further information would you need? _____

   _____

2. Tabitha promised to go out with Jeremy tonight, but when she got home she found out her mom needed her to help out in their family's restaurant. When she broke her date with Jeremy, he told her she was untrustworthy and had no right to break her promise to him.

   Do you agree with Jeremy?_____

   Strongly disagree   **Sort of disagree**   **Not enough information**   **Sort of agree**   **Strongly agree**

   What further information would you need? _____

   _____

3. Michael found a twenty dollar bill on the floor at the supermarket where he works. He spent it that night at the movies.

   Do you agree with what Michael did?_____

   Strongly disagree   **Sort of disagree**   **Not enough information**   **Sort of agree**   **Strongly agree**

   What further information would you need? _____

   _____

Catechism paragraphs 1803–1876

Have you noticed that it gets harder to avoid temptations and sin as you get older? St. Paul even wrote about this problem centuries ago. He said, "For I do not do the good I want, but the evil I do not want is what I do. Now if I do what I do not want, it is no longer I that do it, but sin that dwells within me" (Romans 7:19-20).

That's a very good description of the effect that original sin has had on all of us ever since our first parents disobeyed God. We know Christ died and rose to save us from sin and that he offers us grace through the sacraments, but we still find ourselves choosing to sin.

The *Catechism* says, "Sin is an offense against reason, truth, and right conscience; it is failure in genuine love for God and neighbor…" (paragraph 1849). The most serious sin is mortal sin, a complete turning away from God. For a sin to be "mortal," there are three requirements:

- The sin must be seriously wrong.
- The person must know it is seriously wrong.
- The person must have freely chosen to commit the sin.

Venial sin is less serious and does not cut us off completely from God, but it does weaken us. We must try to avoid them, and should confess them and do penance to make up for them.

True life in Christ cannot be sin-filled. A sinful life is a life of **vice,** a life of habitually wrong decisions and acts. A good life is a life of virtue. Virtues are good acts you do so often they become part of who you are and how you live. The *Catechism* says, "[Virtue] allows the person not only to perform good acts, but to give the best of himself" (paragraph 1803). We all start out with basic human virtues that keep us balanced and able to do good. Because of human virtues, though you may feel sinful, you *are* also good!

There are three *theological virtues* that come from God and lead us to God. They are the virtues of *faith,* by which you believe in God; *hope,* by which you long to be with God and trust you will be with him; and *charity,* by which you love God above all things and love your neighbor as yourself. Sin and virtue live within each of us. Which do you choose?

Know Our Catholic Belief

There are four human virtues on which all the other human virtues hinge. They are called the *cardinal virtues: prudence,* which makes us tend to make good choices; *justice*, by which we tend to be fair; *fortitude,* which is the strength to overcome fear; and *temperance,* which helps us to use moderation in our use of things. Humans start out with those four virtues, and with the right upbringing and training, they grow and other human virtues grow up around them. Then, God steps in with grace, which purifies and raises these human virtues.

Word Search

Answer the questions below, and search for them in the puzzle grid. The remaining letters, written in order, will spell a hidden message.

```
W  H  H  J  L  D  I  C  L  S  G
L  T  H  U  A  E  F  D  A  L  E
A  I  O  S  T  C  O  C  N  L  N
I  A  R  T  R  N  R  H  I  E  U
N  F  I  I  O  A  T  A  D  W  I
E  V  G  C  M  L  I  R  R  D  N
V  I  I  E  O  A  T  I  A  Y  E
O  R  N  C  U  B  U  T  C  C  H
H  T  A  O  E  O  D  Y  S  E  O
S  U  L  E  C  N  E  D  U  R  P
T  E  M  P  E  R  A  N  C  E  E
```

1. Virtues keep us _____.
2. _____ is the name for the four human virtues.
3. _____ is the theological virtue of love of God and neighbor.
4. St. Paul said, "Sin _____ within me."
5. _____ is the theological virtue of belief in God.
6. _____ is the virtue that strengthens us to overcome fear.
7. Sin is failure in _____ love for God and neighbor.
8. The theological virtue of trust that we will be with God in heaven is _____.
9. The virtue that helps us to be fair is _____.
10. _____ sin completely turns us away from God.
11. _____ sin is the sin of our first parents.
12. _____ is the virtue that helps us make good choices.
13. Christ offers us grace through the _____.
14. Moderation in our use of things is known as _____.
15. _____ sin is a less serious sin that we should still avoid.
16. A sinful life is a life of _____.
17. A good act that we do often is a _____.

HIDDEN MESSAGE:

_____.

The Person and Society

Catechism paragraphs 1877–1927

Think about the groups to which you belong. You began in a family, but by now you've branched out to be part of quite a few other groups of people.

The Church is present in every land on earth, so her members are members of many different civil societies. The Church offers basic ideals and principles to guide all societies.

Different communities or societies have different rules and different reasons for existing, but each group ought to put the *good of human beings* above any other reason for being in existence. No society should ever make it difficult for people to live lives of virtue, and no society should obstruct human freedom.

The Church often uses the term "the common good" when teaching about the relationships of people in any society. By "the common good," the Church means "the sum total of social conditions which allow people, either as groups or as individuals, to reach their fulfillment more fully and more easily" (*Catechism,* paragraphs 1906, 1924).

The Church stands up and speaks out on behalf of all people all over the world. She reminds us of the *dignity of each human person* and asks us if all our institutions promote human dignity and improve human conditions.

The Church also speaks out to the world community, reminding all nations that, though each one is to promote the common good of their own society, there should be international organizations that promote the common good for the whole human family.

Your personal dignity is shared by every other person on the planet. When you are hurt or are refused your rights, all are hurt in the Body of Christ. When anyone else is degraded or demeaned, in the end, it hurts you, too.

Know Our Catholic Belief

In order to have the common good, three elements are required:
- respect for and promotion of the basic rights of each person,
- prosperity or development of the spiritual and material goods of society, and
- peace and security of all in the group.

Evaluate Your Own Groups

Fill in the chart below for five different groups to which you belong (for example, family, parish, scout troop, sports team, town, or city).

Groups	Example of how each member is respected and given rights	Example of how members prosper spiritually and materially	Example of how each member has peace and security

Catechism paragraphs 1928–1948

Over the years the Church has needed to speak out on many issues regarding how nations and institutions have failed to provide for the common good or to exercise authority over groups of people.

Based on the Gospel teachings of Jesus, and spoken in response to problems and offenses that have arisen, the Church has developed principles of *social justice.*

A society can be sure it is a just society when it provides conditions that make it possible for all groups and members in the society to receive what they have a right to.

What do you know about some of the conditions of people in the world and in our own country? Do all people of different races get along? What about people of different religions? Do all workers have good conditions in their workplaces? Are all workers given enough pay? Does everyone have a home? Does everyone have enough to eat? You can see that social justice is a lot of work and a difficult challenge for any society.

The first thing a just society must have is *respect* for each human person and a concern for the rights of each person. A society must never lose sight of the dignity of each human being.

Next, a just society must strive for *equality.* Certainly, people are different and have different gifts and needs, but you know that some people or groups are drastically poorer than others or are treated much less fairly. The Church points out the sinfulness of such inequalities and urges us to work to bring them to an end.

Finally, social justice can be achieved if people work toward *solidarity,* or "social charity." We can first see solidarity when people begin to share their profits and goods and begin to negotiate to receive and give rights. Solidarity leads people to share with each other, to talk to each other, to share not only material goods but also spiritual goods.

Know Our Catholic Tradition

The Gospel of Jesus promotes a just society. Great doctors of the Church like St. Thomas Aquinas and St. Augustine; great popes like Leo XIII, Paul VI, and John Paul II; and groups of bishops in areas like Africa, South America, and the United States have all contributed over the centuries to the Church's social justice teaching.

Dreaming Dreams of Justice

What dreams of social justice do you have? In the clouds below, write *four* different dreams you have for the future of the world. On the earth below the clouds, write *four specific* steps you can take now or very soon that would begin to make that dream come true. (For example: If I dream of a world where people of all races get along, I could begin by learning something positive about a race other than my own, or by meeting a person of another race.)

I dream

I dream

I dream

I dream

The Steps I Can Take

Loving God

Catechism paragraphs 2083–2195

From the beginning, God has planted a **natural law** in each person. It's the law within us that tells us what is right and wrong. From that law, all moral rules and civil laws were developed. Then God began to reveal his Law. To this day, we have the commandments. In Jesus, we have a new commandment of love, which does not replace the **Ten Commandments** but teaches us what they mean for people who are "blessed." Jesus expressed God's Law in the **Beatitudes.**

In the commandments given by God, we learn how we are to think of God, speak of God, and worship God. The first Great Commandment is: *You shall love the Lord your God with all your heart, with all your soul, with all your mind, and with all your strength.* There is absolutely no doubt what this means! We are to put God first.

1. *"I am the Lord your God: You shall not have strange gods before me."* This commandment tells us how God wants us to think of him. Do you think of God as a person who loves you and gives you life? Do you pray to him, really talk and listen to him? Do you trust him or do you believe in superstitions and magic?

2. *"You shall not take the name of the Lord your God in vain."* This commandment tells us how God wants us to speak of him. Your language says a lot about how much you love and honor God.

3. *"Remember to keep holy the Lord's Day."* This tells how God wants us to worship him. Do you worship God at a Saturday evening or Sunday Eucharistic Liturgy and set aside time to relax? God wants us to worship as part of a community. He wants us to rest one day out of seven in order to be refreshed and renewed and ready to serve him.

Know Our Catholic Tradition

The Ten Commandments (or Decalogue) are often shown carved on tablets divided three on one side and seven on the other. In this symbolic way, we remember the first Great Commandment sums up the first three of the Ten Commandments, and the second Great Commandment sums up the rest.

Honest Words to God

Use the questions under each of the commandments in Lesson 30 to write a three-part letter to God. In it, tell him your thoughts about each of the first three commandments—what they mean, why they're difficult sometimes, how you've done with them, and what help you need from him.

Dear God,

Catechism paragraphs 2197–2257

Have you ever wished you didn't have so many rules to keep? Do you think it'll be great to be your own boss and not have to listen to parents and teachers all the time?

Of course you've thought all these things! Obedience isn't easy, and it seems to get more difficult for people your age. The Fourth Commandment, *"Honor your father and your mother,"* isn't usually anyone's favorite to talk about, but it's the first way we keep the second Great Commandment, the one that says, "You shall love your neighbor as you love yourself."

Both the Old and New Testaments are very concerned with how parents and their children get along. Check out the Book of Proverbs sometime and see all the advice in it for you and for your parents— especially your dad. Or read how Abraham treated Isaac, how Isaac treated his twins Jacob and Esau, and how Jacob raised his twelve boys.

It is clear when you read Scripture that parents and children do not always agree but that there is a strong bond that links them. In a letter to some early Christians, St. Paul wrote: "Children, obey your parents in everything, for this is your acceptable duty in the Lord. Fathers, do not provoke your children, or they may lose heart" (Colossians 3:20-21).

The Fourth Commandment is a two-way street. It is concerned with how parents and children treat one another. It is concerned with how each family member carries out his or her duties in a Christian home.

This commandment asks *anyone* who is in charge to look at his or her style of leadership. What are you like when you are in charge of younger children or of a group of people your own age? All leaders, of any age, are to *remember that their authority comes from God.* How does God lead us? With love. No leader should bully, harm, frighten, neglect, or mislead anyone in his or her charge.

Beyond our homes and classrooms, and when we're not at home and school anymore, what kind of authority is in our lives? It is our duty as Christians and as citizens to obey all legitimate authority. We obey elected and appointed public officials, and it is the responsibility of all state and civil authority to respect the rights and dignity of each person. We obey Church leaders, and we also respect these people and the offices they hold.

Know Our Catholic Belief

If any person in authority directs us to do something that is against God's Law, we do not have to obey. In fact, we must not obey any direction that is not morally right.

Scriptures for Parents and Kids

Look up the passages below and write what you might say if you were there.

Genesis 22:1–12
If you were Isaac, what would you say to your father after this happened?

_____

_____

_____

_____

Genesis 25:24-34, 27:1–40
If you were Jacob, what would you really want to say to your father, and how would you explain to him how you had treated your twin brother?

_____

_____

_____

_____

Genesis 37:2–10
If you were one of the older brothers, what might you say to your father about your brother Joseph?

_____

_____

_____

_____

Human Life Is Sacred

Catechism paragraphs 2258–2330

The Fifth Commandment, *"You shall not kill,"* tells us that *all human life is sacred.*

Another way to look at keeping this commandment is to always ask ourselves as we consider how we treat any human being—including ourselves—"How does the Creator want me to treat this person he has created?"

Deliberate killing—murder—is absolutely forbidden. The only time a person may kill another person is in legitimate defense, when his or her own or others' lives are threatened. The life of every unborn baby is sacred, so during pregnancy all care must be taken to protect the unborn child, even when it is still a tiny embryo. That embryo is a human person. **Abortion**—the killing of an unborn baby—is wrong.

The lives of seriously disabled people and very old or ill people are also sacred, so **euthanasia,** ending life as a way to end suffering, is forbidden. It is even wrong to put someone to death as a punishment for a capital crime such as murder. God is the author of all life, and the end of each life is to be in his hands.

We must also take care of our own lives. Suicide is a terrible waste of any life and is against the Fifth Commandment. Anyone who thinks of suicide should seek help and reach out to those who love him or her. It is also against the Fifth Commandment to do anything to harm our bodies. This includes smoking, improperly using drugs or alcohol, or harming our health in any way.

Another sin against this commandment is **scandal.** Scandal is the deliberate leading of another person to do evil. This form of killing is spiritual and is a serious sin.

Know Our Catholic Belief

War has deadly effects even when war is not fought.
The worst is the arms race—the stockpiling of nuclear weapons.
Even when these weapons are not used, they are taking lives by taking money and resources away from the production of food and goods.

My Life Is Sacred

You are worth so much that Jesus died on the cross for you! Take the following inventory to get a look at how sacred your life is:

List your top three physical gifts.

1._____

2._____

3._____

List your top three spiritual gifts.

1._____

2._____

3._____

Explain how you can use any one of those physical or spiritual gifts to contribute to the common good in some way.

_____

_____

_____

List three things that are average about you.	List three things that are unique or unusual about you.
1._____	1._____
2._____	2._____
3._____	3._____

Write a prayer of thanks to God for your life. Be specific.

_____

_____

_____

Made in God's Image

Catechism paragraphs 2331–2400, 2514–2533

Two commandments are concerned with our sexuality. The Sixth Commandment is, *"You shall not commit **adultery**,"* and the Ninth Commandment is, *"You shall not **covet** your neighbor's wife."*

Both of these commandments tell married people to be faithful to their marriage vows, which are made for life and are never to be broken. They promise to live together as husband and wife all their lives and not to leave each other for different partners or to be married to more than one partner at the same time. They promise to accept any children that God sends them and to do nothing artificial to prevent the conception of children.

Of course, these two commandments have much to tell you before you are married, or even if you never marry. Married or not, we are all sexual beings and God's Law directs how we use this gift.

We look to Christ as our model in keeping these commandments, and we find in him the virtue of chastity. All of us are to be chaste, that is, to be at peace with our sexuality, using it only as it is intended within our particular state of life, and to be respectful of our own and of others' sexuality.

The chaste person works to master his or her thoughts, words, and actions regarding sexuality. Sins against chastity and the Sixth Commandment include masturbation, sexual intercourse outside of marriage, pornography, and homosexual actions.

The Ninth Commandment tells us not to "covet" anyone to whom we are not married. This has a lot to do with how we think about people and their sexuality, how we act toward others, and how we encourage them to act toward us. This commandment is kept by the beatitude Jesus gave us: "Blessed are the pure in heart."

In all our behavior, style of clothes, speech, and action we should be modest, doing nothing to call attention to our sexuality in an inappropriate way and guarding our own sexual dignity.

Know Our Catholic Belief

With our bodies we are able to participate in the miracle of creation. God has given both male and female bodies great powers and great gifts. Whether you are male or female, you should thank God for the gift of your body.

Clues and Transfers

Refer to Lesson 33 to fill in each blank below. When a line has a number beneath it, transfer that letter to the blank marked with that number at the bottom of the page. When you are finished, the transfers will spell an important message.

1. God has given both __ __ __ __ and __ __ __ __ __ __ bodies
                          3   14   9

   __ __ __ __ __ powers and gifts.
    6 24   12

2. The Sixth Commandment is "You shall not __ __ __ __ __ __
                                           26   16

   __ __ __ __ __ __ __ __."
     8   11 28

3. The Ninth Commandment is "You shall not __ __ __ __ __ your neighbor's
                                         7   18

   __ __ __ __."
     17

4. We __ __ __ __ to Christ as our model, and we find the
       19 10 5

   virtue of __ __ __ __ __ __ __ __ .
           2   21

5. The Ninth Commandment is kept by the beatitude, "__ __ __ __ __ __ __
                                 25   27

   are the __ __ __ __ in heart."
        23

6. When we are __ __ __ __ __ __ in all our behavior, we guard our
              22

   sexual __ __ __ __ __ __ __.
         15   1

7. These two commandments tell married people to be __ __ __ __ __ __ __ __
                                        20   13

   to their vows, but we must keep these commandments even if we

   __ __ __ __ __ marry.
    4

THE MESSAGE:

__ __ __ __ __ __ __ __ __ __ __ __ __ __ __ __ __ __
 1 2 3 4 5   6 7 8   9 10 11   12 13 14   15 16 17 18

__ __ __ __ __ __ __ __ __ __.
19 20 21   22 23 24   25 26 27 28

Catechism paragraphs 2401–2463, 2534–2557

The Seventh Commandment says, *"You shall not steal,"* and the Tenth says, *"You shall not covet anything that belongs to your neighbor."* Both tell us how we are to own and use property. Now that you are older and starting to make more of your own money, you will find yourself more aware of the problems these two commandments address.

When you remember all things come from God, it helps you know how to view your property. The Seventh Commandment says you have the right to own property and use what you need of God's gifts. No one may steal your property, and you may not steal his or hers. You also don't have the right to steal words or music from published books, to copy schoolwork, or to cheat someone out of money you owe him or her. Anything taken unlawfully must be returned, or its rightful owner must be given its full value. That's called **restitution.**

The Seventh Commandment is also concerned with labor. Slavery is a sin against this commandment and so is refusing to pay people just wages for their work. It is also wrong not to give an employer a full day's work for the pay you receive or to "cut corners" on a job. Every gift of creation comes from God, and human beings are the stewards of all these gifts. We are to care for them, preserve resources for the future, and see that they are justly distributed. God's gifts were given for everyone, so poverty is a sin against the Seventh Commandment. We must each do what we can in charity to help those who have less than we do.

The Tenth Commandment tells us not to covet goods. It means we can't be so full of **envy** that we're sad because someone else has nice things, or that we are willing to do anything to get those things! It also commands us not to be greedy, amassing all we can with no regard for others.

Jesus knows how necessary money and possessions are, but he also knows how dangerous they can be. Once he said, "It is easier for a camel to go through the eye of a needle than for someone who is rich to enter the kingdom of God" (Matthew 19:24).

You can have all you need, but don't let your possessions keep you out of heaven!

Know Our Catholic Belief

Jesus told us in the first Beatitude to be "poor in spirit." He didn't mean that we have to be poor but that our inner selves should not be enslaved by things we own. Have you ever been so caught up in a new "thing" you've gotten that you couldn't think of anything else? People who are poor in spirit don't put their possessions ahead of their friends. They don't put making money ahead of living good lives and loving their families.

Crossword Puzzle

Use Lesson 34 to help you
solve this puzzle.

ACROSS

2. To want something so much we are willing to do anything to get it is called _____.

4. We may not steal words or music from _____ books.

6. Returning what has been stolen is called _____.

9. We must work to preserve _____ for the future.

12. Money is necessary, but it also can be _____.

13. We must do what we can in _____ to help the poor.

14. We may not _____ someone out of money we owe him or her.

15. Employers must pay _____ wages for work that people do.

DOWN

1. We should never put our _____ ahead of our friends.

3. God meant for his gifts to be _____ distributed.

5. It is wrong to "cut _____" on a job.

7. The Seventh Commandment says, "You shall not _____."

8. Amassing all we can with no regard for others is called being _____.

10. All gifts come from God, and we are the _____ of these gifts.

11. Jesus said it was easier for a camel to go through the eye of a _____ than for a rich person to enter heaven.

Catechism paragraphs 2464–2513

The Eighth Commandment is, *"You shall not bear false witness against your neighbor."* It deals with speaking the truth.

Everyone wants people to tell the truth about them. You do, don't you? Don't you feel trapped and helpless when you find out someone has gone around talking about you, saying things that aren't true or are only half true? This is what bearing false witness means. The worst kind of false witness damages or ruins someone's **reputation.** This happened to Jesus often, including at his final trial.

How careful are you about how you speak of others? Even if we speak the truth, if it damages a person's good name, it's against the Eighth Commandment.

Lying of any kind is forbidden. We need to guard ourselves against becoming dishonest or hypocritical. If we do lie about someone and cause public harm to someone's reputation we must make **reparation.** This is very difficult! It is much easier to give back an object we've stolen from someone than it is to return his or her good name or pay him or her for it.

The Eighth Commandment also deals with secrets. Secrets or personal matters told in confidence may not be repeated.

This is especially true for people who must hear personal matters as part of their profession—priests, counselors, attorneys, and others with similar professions.

The Eighth Commandment doesn't just tell us not to lie, it also encourages us to *speak and live the truth.* The *Catechism* includes much discussion of the social communications media—the press, radio, TV, and other electronic media. We have wonderful ways to disseminate the truth all over the world. We should use them wisely and honestly.

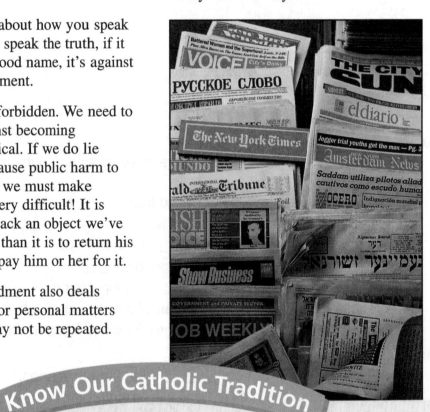

Know Our Catholic Tradition

You might be surprised to know the *Catechism* also includes a section on sacred art in the article about the Eighth Commandment. It praises artists who by the work of their hands express the truth and beauty of God. We are all called to express God's truth and beauty by the way we live our lives in Christ.

Advice Column

You are the advice columnist for a teen magazine. Answer these letters, basing your answers on what you know about the Eighth Commandment.

Dear Gifts,

_____

_____

_____

_____

_____

_____

_____

Dear Wise One,

A bunch of us guys have had a lot of fun on the Internet, but now our parents are making us stop. What's so wrong about sending e-mail to girls who are real lonely telling them we like them a lot? We even sent pictures of guys and told them they were pictures of us. We're helping these girls feel better about themselves. Don't you think our parents are wrong to stop us?

Gifts to Girls

Dear Wise One,

I told everybody a lie about my friend when I was mad at her. And everybody believed me! Now, the lie is all around school, and her reputation is ruined. I want her for my friend. How can I make this up to her?

Sadder and Wiser

Dear Sadder,

_____

_____

_____

_____

_____

Section Three
Review

Mark a "T" in front of any statement that is true. Mark an "F" in front of false statements and then CHANGE THE STATEMENT TO MAKE IT TRUE.

___ 1. Free will does not give us the right to do whatever we please.

___ 2. The Church does not interfere with how different nations treat their citizens.

___ 3. It is not really possible for all people to expect to get their rights.

___ 4. Natural law is the law within us that tells us what is right and wrong.

___ 5. All human life—both before it is born and after it is very old or ill—is sacred.

___ 6. The Sixth and Ninth Commandments are only for married people.

___ 7. Jesus taught that money and possessions are not really necessary and that we should all be as poor as we can be.

Circle the best answer for each question below.

1. You must follow your conscience _____.
   a. instead of listening to anyone
   b. only when no one is around to help you decide
   c. if you have gathered enough information and are sure it is informed and correct

2. Faith, hope, and love are _____.
   a. the theological virtues   b. the cardinal virtues   c. human virtues

3. Social conditions that make it possible for people to receive what they have a right to constitutes _____.
   a. a just society   b. more money for everyone   c. solidarity

4. We can tell from reading Scripture that _____.
   a. parents and children got along until modern times
   b. parents are always right
   c. parents and children do not always agree but still have a strong bond

5. A form of spiritual killing that leads another person to do evil is called _____.
   a. scandal   b. abortion   c. euthanasia

6. When we are at peace with our sexuality and use it as intended we are _____.
   a. modest   b. married   c. chaste

7. When we make restitution, we _____.
   a. confess that we have stolen something
   b. give back what we've stolen   c. preserve resources

Section Four
We Catholics Pray

The fourth part of the *Catechism* is titled "Christian Prayer." All the other parts lead up to this shortest, but most personal, part. In it, we consider how we express our relationship with God in prayer.

This section of your book will invite you to look into your own heart and to open yourself to conversation with God.

Catechism paragraphs 2558–2622

Have you discovered what kind of pray-er you are yet? What have you learned about prayer? What kinds of prayers do you like to pray? When is your best time to pray? A lot of young people report they like to pray at night when they're alone, before they go to sleep. You can just talk to God then in your own words while lying in the dark.

"Is *that* real prayer?" you might ask. You might not think it is. You aren't using Church words, and God doesn't answer.

How do you know you aren't just talking to yourself? Because of God's plan of salvation. Remember? He did all he did *for you.* Sure, this has been everyone's plan of salvation, but God would have done it just for you. Really. It is God's plan for you.

So, whether it's in the dark, or wherever you like to spend time alone thinking, God is calling you. That's God speaking to your heart. Really. And that's God listening.

The *Catechism* says that "God tirelessly calls each person…" (paragraph 2591). You are not just called when you are alone. You are called every minute—called to live in the truth, called to keep the commandments, called to celebrate, called to be fair, called to be generous, called to be chaste, called to share your possessions, called to. . . . Now, how can anybody possibly do all that alone? How can anybody possibly do all that without help?

Christians turn to God for that help. They also turn to each other within their Christian communities. So we pray together, too. And we pray for each other.

Know Our Catholic Tradition

What do you do when it's hard to pray? It's easy to get distracted. It's easy to say you're too busy, or to let someone talk you out of praying. Sometimes you even wonder if God hears your prayers. At these times, we should be more faithful to prayer than ever and ask the Holy Spirit to help. Remember, St. Paul wrote that the Holy Spirit will come to help us when we do not know how to pray (see Romans 8:26).

A Personal Prayer Survey

Write honest answers to all the questions below. Spend some quiet time really thinking about your answers and what they say about you and your friendship with God.

My best times of day to pray: _____

My favorite vocal prayers or kinds of prayers: _____

_____

Some things I always mention to God when I pray: _____

_____

Some things I often ask for from God: _____

_____

I always thank God for: _____

_____

_____

Some questions I have for God about the world: _____

_____

_____

Some things I have heard God tell me within my heart: _____

_____

_____

Some things in my life for which I really need God's help: _____

_____

_____

I tell God about these fears I have: _____

_____

_____

Catechism paragraphs 2623–2649

Whether you are praying in your own words, or praying vocal prayers with a group of people, your prayer will be made up of one or more of the basic forms of prayer. These prayer forms are what the Holy Spirit has taught the whole Church: **blessing** and **adoration, petition, intercession, thanksgiving,** and **praise.**

Prayers of blessing and adoration are the most basic of prayers. Remember, though, that you don't begin by *asking for things.* You begin by *seeing what you already have.* God has already showered you with blessings, and now you bless God in return.

Blessing is like a two-way conversation with God. It is immediately followed by adoration, which is our recognition that we are creatures, and God is almighty and all-powerful, our creator and the source of all life and blessings.

The second basic prayer form is the prayer of petition, the prayer of asking for the things you need. Before that, however, petition first *asks for forgiveness.*

You can see why the Holy Spirit teaches us to ask for forgiveness right after moving us to blessing and adoration. As you honestly realize how great and good God is, you also honestly see how you have failed to love him and trust him.

After this, your petitions ask for your needs, but true prayer doesn't ask for anything extra, only for the things we need to live our lives in Christ.

Prayer of intercession is the third prayer form. Like petition, intercession turns to God with needs, but in this form you pray *for the needs of others.* You look beyond yourself and recognize what other people need.

The fourth form of prayer the Spirit teaches us is the prayer of thanksgiving. Every gift from God, every answer to prayer (even the answer "no"), should bring a response of thanksgiving from you. Prayers of thanks are so basic in the Church that we call our central liturgical celebration "Eucharist." The word *Eucharist* means "thanksgiving." Our greatest thanks to God is for his greatest gift—his own Son, Jesus.

Prayer of praise is the fifth basic form of prayer. This form of prayer raises words and thoughts of wonder and awe toward God *just because he is God.* Prayers of praise recognize that you would give God glory, even if he never gave you anything at all! God is worth praising just because he is God.

Know Our Catholic Belief

You do not need to label which form of prayers you are praying, but it is good to recognize that there are different forms. Pray to God in all five of these forms at some time. Often, people discover they neglect one form or another: They forget to say "thanks," or they fail to ask for forgiveness.

Word Search

Solve the clues below and find the words in the letter grid. After all the words are circled, the remaining letters, written in order, will spell an important message.

```
S  P  G  O  D  H  A  R  T  X  E
A  S  E  J  E  S  U  S  C  S  S
E  H  E  T  O  W  E  R  E  R  E
D  U  G  N  I  S  S  E  L  B  Y
Y  O  C  U  E  T  W  H  G  E  I
D  T  V  H  H  V  I  T  E  Y  M
A  D  O  R  A  T  I  O  N  O  A
E  N  C  Y  B  R  L  G  N  N  E
R  E  A  S  I  S  I  I  R  D  V
L  N  L  P  R  A  I  S  E  O  I
A  G  S  L  A  B  E  L  T  S  F
```

1. _____ is the prayer that recognizes we are creatures of an all-powerful God.
2. We begin by seeing what we_____ have from God.
3. In the prayer of intercession, we look _____ ourselves.
4. A prayer that is like a two-way conversation with God is _____.
5. _____ means "thanksgiving."
6. We should not ask for anything _____ from God, just for what we need.
7. The *Catechism* mentions _____ basic prayer forms.
8. In the prayer of petition, we first ask for _____.
9. _____ is the name of God's greatest gift to us.
10. We do not really need to _____ which forms of prayer we are praying, but it is good to recognize them.
11. We should try not to _____ any form of prayer.
12. Intercession is prayer for _____.
13. The prayer of asking for things we need is called _____.
14. Prayer to God just because he is God is called _____.
15. The _____ teaches us to pray.
16. _____ prayer is prayed aloud.

HIDDEN MESSAGE: _____.

38 Hail, Mary

Catechism paragraphs 2673–2682

It's important for you to know the place Mary has in the Church's life of prayer. Mary's whole life is a model of prayer. Her "yes" to God's request for her to be his mother was a complete turning of her heart and will over to God.

You've been praying at least one traditional prayer to Mary since you were quite young—the Hail Mary:

Hail, Mary. We use the same words the angel Gabriel used to greet Mary at the Annunciation, knowing it is a greeting from God to her.

Full of grace, the Lord is with you. Gabriel said these two phrases to Mary, too. God filled Mary full of his life from the moment of her conception. Now, as the mother of Jesus, God is truly with her, living in her body and her soul.

Blessed are you among women and blessed is the fruit of your womb, Jesus. Now we take up words first spoken by Mary's cousin, Elizabeth, when Mary went to visit her. Among all the women of all time, Mary has been chosen to be the mother of the Savior.

Holy Mary, Mother of God. Elizabeth said, "Why has this happened to me, that the mother of my Lord comes to me" (Luke 1:43)? We speak these words with the same realization of how blessed we are to have such a mother available to help us.

Pray for us sinners, now and at the hour of our death. Here we can see that we are praying to Mary so that she will pray for us. She has no power of her own to answer prayers, but she is Queen of Heaven and close to the throne of God. We ask her now to lead us from death into eternal life.

Know Our Catholic Belief

All prayers to Mary are centered on Jesus Christ. We do not worship Mary. Really, we pray in communion with Mary, and our prayers have two parts to them. First, all traditional Catholic prayers to Mary give praise to God for the great things he has done for her and through her for all human beings. Second, traditional prayers raise up requests for help and words of praise to Mary, the mother of God.

Clues and Transfers

To fill in each blank below, refer to Lesson 38 and to the things you've learned about Mary elsewhere. When a line has a number beneath it, transfer that letter to the blank marked with that number at the bottom of the page. When you are finished, the transfers will spell an important message.

1. Mary's whole life is a __ __ __ __ __ of prayer.
   10   24 5

   Her "__ __ __" to God was complete.
   13 28

2. We do not __ __ __ __ __ __ __ Mary; we pray
   9 22 31   1

   in __ __ __ __ __ __ __ __ __ with her.
   17 25   30   26

3. Mary became our mother when Jesus gave her to __ __ __ __ as
   27   19

   he was dying on the __ __ __ __ __ .
   2   29

4. We call Mary __ __ __ __ because she is full of __ __ __ __ __ .
   4   15 3   21

5. We ask Mary to pray for us __ __ __ __ __ __ __, now and at the hour of
   7   16 6

   our __ __ __ __ __, and to lead us into __ __ __ __ __ __ __ life.
   18 11 8   23 20 12   14

THE MESSAGE:

__ __ __ __ __ __ __ __ __ __ __ __ __ __ __ __
1 2 3 4 5 6 7   8 9   10 11 12 13 14 15 16

__ __ __ __ __ __ __ __ __ __ __ __ __ __ __.
17 18 19 20 21 22 23 24 25 26 27 28 29 30 31

The Lord's Prayer

Catechism paragraphs 2759–2865

All Christian Churches pray the Lord's Prayer—it's the one prayer we all know and can pray together.

Many saints and scholars have meditated on the words of the Lord's Prayer and have written sermons, essays, or books about it. We pray it today as people have prayed it ever since the Church began. It is the most basic and most perfectly constructed prayer we have in the Church.

Here's what the great scholar and doctor of the Church, St. Thomas Aquinas, wrote:

> The Lord's Prayer is the most perfect of prayers. . . . In it we ask, not only for all the things we can rightly desire, but also in the sequence that they should be desired. This prayer not only teaches us to ask for things, but also in what order we should desire them.
> Quoted in the *Catechism*, paragraph 2763

So let's look at the order in which things are requested in the Lord's Prayer:

1. We ask that God's name be revered and honored.

2. We ask for the coming of God's kingdom.

3. We ask that the will of God would be done on earth the way it is done in heaven.

4. We ask for the material things we need for the day.

5. We ask for forgiveness—but only as much as we are open to God's grace to forgive others!

6. We ask for help to stay away from things that tempt us to sin.

7. We ask for protection from evil.

The prayer we say today is closest to the version in the Gospel of Matthew, but have you ever prayed the Lord's Prayer with people who belong to a Protestant religion? They put an extra ending on it, don't they? They pray: "… but deliver us from evil. For thine is the kingdom and the power and the glory forever and ever. Amen." Why do they pray that? Why don't we?

As it turns out, we do, but only during the Eucharistic Liturgy. Pay attention for it the next time you are at Mass. After we all say, "but deliver us from evil," the celebrant goes on to say a prayer that begins, "Deliver us, Lord, from every evil…," and at the end of that prayer, we all answer, "For the kingdom, the power, and the glory are yours, now and forever."

Know Our Catholic Tradition

Did Jesus really say the Lord's Prayer in the exact same words we use to pray it today? Well, for one thing, he prayed it in Aramaic, so what we are praying is a translation. If you look in Scripture, however, you'll find that both Matthew and Luke reported that Jesus taught the apostles a prayer. The versions, however, are slightly different. You can look them up in Matthew 6:9-13 and Luke 11:2-4.

Make it Personal

Jesus wanted us not only to learn the words of the Lord's Prayer, but more importantly, to learn from it *how* we should pray. Write a prayer for each of these requests that is in your own words. Mention specific needs that reflect today's world in your own life and the lives of the people for whom you care.

For the things I need for today:

_____

_____

_____

_____

_____

_____

That God's kingdom will come:

_____

_____

_____

_____

_____

_____

That we on earth will *do* what God wants:

_____

_____

_____

_____

_____

_____

Help me stay away from:

_____

_____

_____

_____

_____

_____

_____

For forgiveness—for me and for those who've hurt me:

_____

_____

_____

_____

_____

_____

Review

Mark a "T" in front of any statement that is true. Mark an "F" in front of any false statement and then change it to make it true.

_____ 1. Prayer in your own words is okay, but it's not real prayer.

_____ 2. God's plan of salvation is for the Church, not for each person individually.

_____ 3. The Holy Spirit teaches us how to pray and prays for us when we don't know how.

_____ 4. We begin prayer by seeing what we need and asking for it.

_____ 5. God won't bless you with anything unless you pray for it first.

_____ 6. We worship Mary the same way we worship God.

_____ 7. Only Catholics pray the Lord's Prayer.

Circle the best answer for each question below.

1. Everyone should pray _____.
   a. at night   b. at a time that is best for them   c. when they need things

2. God calls us to pray _____.
   a. every minute   b. once a week on Sunday   c. when we are alone

3. When we get distracted and have trouble praying, we should _____.
   a. stop   b. ask the Holy Spirit for help   c. ask God to forgive us

4. Prayer of blessing is immediately followed by _____.
   a. adoration   b. more blessings from God   c. intercession

5. We should thank God _____.
   a. when we finally get what we asked for   b. before we ask for more
   c. even when his answer is "no"

6. Mary's whole life _____.
   a. is a model of prayer   b. was full of sorrow   c. was planned by God so she had no choices

7. The Lord's Prayer not only tells us to ask for things but also _____.
   a. the order in which we should ask for them
   b. exactly what words to say   c. when to pray

Glossary

abortion The act of killing an unborn baby.

absolution A blessing given as a sign of God's forgiveness.

adoration A form of prayer that tells God we know he is the all-powerful Creator from whom all things come.

adultery Being unfaithful to one's marriage vows.

altar A table of sacrifice. Table on which the Eucharistic Liturgy is celebrated. It is always either made of stone or contains a stone in its center in which are embedded some relics of saints.

ambo The lectern from which Scripture is proclaimed at the Eucharistic Liturgy.

Anointing of the Sick Sacrament that gives healing to the sick.

apostolic A characteristic of the Church, which was founded on the apostles by Jesus Christ.

archbishop A bishop given the special honor of heading an archdiocese.

archdiocese A geographic area that has a large number of Catholics, headed by an archbishop.

Ascension The return of Jesus to his Father in heaven, celebrated 40 days after Easter.

Assumption Doctrine that teaches us Mary was taken into heaven, body and soul, after she died.

Baptism The sacrament of initiation into a new life in Christ that makes us members of the Church.

baptismal promises Promises each person makes at Baptism. We renew these promises each year at Easter and when we receive the sacrament of Confirmation.

baptistry Area in a church building where baptisms are celebrated.

Beatitudes Eight ways to be blessed or happy, listed by Jesus in Matthew 5:1-12 as a way to describe the Law of God.

Benediction of the Blessed Sacrament A devotional ceremony in which the Eucharist is adored and the faithful are given a solemn blessing.

bishop A priest who receives the highest degree of Holy Orders so he can lead an area of the Church called a diocese. The Twelve Apostles were the first bishops of the Church.

blessing A form of prayer that praises God for what we have already received and asks him to continue to grant goodness.

cantor Liturgical leader of song.

cardinal Ordinarily, a bishop who has been given the special honor of belonging to the college of cardinals, the group that elects a new pope when needed.

catholic Universal. A characteristic of the Church, which is catholic because she transcends time and geography and is for all people.

celebrant One of the titles of the priest who presides at the Eucharistic Liturgy.

chalice The cup (usually gold or gold-plated) that holds the Precious Blood of the Eucharist.

Glossary

character A permanent spiritual sign. At both Baptism and Confirmation we receive a special character, so these sacraments cannot be repeated.

chastity The virtue of honoring our sexuality as a special gift from God. Also, a vow made by religious brothers, sisters, and priests to never marry.

chrism The oil used to anoint a person into a share of Christ's priesthood. This oil is used in Baptism, Confirmation, and Holy Orders.

Christ Title for Jesus that means "anointed."

ciborium Covered cup or dish that holds the Body of Christ.

communion of saints Doctrine that teaches us we are united as one Church with everyone on earth, the saints in heaven, and the souls in purgatory.

Confirmation Sacrament of initiation that completes Baptism by giving the gifts of the Holy Spirit.

conscience The power inside each person to know what is right and what is wrong.

consecrate The act of changing the bread and wine into the Body and Blood of Christ.

corporal The large white cloth spread in the center of the altar where the Eucharist will be placed at Mass.

counsel The gift of the Holy Spirit that helps us seek good advice from others and give good advice when asked. Also called right judgment.

covenant A solemn promise two people or groups of people make to each other.

covet To want something that does not belong to you.

deacon Man ordained with the third degree of Holy Orders to be of special service to the Church.

diocese A group of parishes in one area, led by a bishop.

Eastern rites Groups of Catholics who acknowledge the authority of the pope but who celebrate the liturgy differently from the Church of the Roman rite. The Eastern rites include the Byzantine, Coptic, Syriac, Armenian, Maronite, and Chaldean rites.

ecumenical council Gathering of the pope and all the bishops of the world for the purpose of defining Church doctrine.

envy Sin of strong resentment and unhappiness over the good fortune or possessions of another.

Eucharist Sacrament in which bread and wine is changed into the Body and Blood of Jesus Christ. This word means "thanksgiving."

eucharistic minister Specially trained lay person who helps the priest distribute Holy Communion at Mass and to the sick and shut-in.

euthanasia Killing of a person who is very ill, elderly, or disabled. Often called "mercy killing," it is a sin against the Fifth Commandment.

evangelical counsels Special virtues described by Jesus in the Gospels. They are poverty, chastity, and obedience. These three are lived as vows by members of religious orders.

evangelize Telling others the Good News of Jesus Christ.

Exsultet A hymn of praise sung during the Eucharistic Liturgy on Holy Saturday night.

Father The First Person in the Holy Trinity. The Father is God, and his mission is to be the Creator.

fear of the Lord Gift of the Holy Spirit that helps us appreciate the wonders of God's love. It is also called wonder and awe.

fortitude Gift of the Holy Spirit that gives inner strength to live our faith in the face of difficulties. It is also called courage.

free will Power given by God to each human being to make choices and decisions.

genuflect To drop to one or both knees as a sign of worship and respect.

grace God's life freely given to us.

heaven The state of eternal life and communion with God.

hell The state of eternal death and separation from God.

hierarchy The leadership of the Church.

holy Full of sanctifying grace. Also a characteristic of the Church. We now can receive grace because Christ saved us from sin.

Holy Orders A sacrament of service that anoints men to special service in the Church as deacons, priests, or bishops.

Holy Spirit The Third Person in the Holy Trinity. The Holy Spirit is God, whose mission is to make us holy.

Holy Trinity Name of the three persons in one God: the Father, the Son, and the Holy Spirit.

hosts Name given to the unleavened bread of the Eucharist that comes in small, round pieces.

Immaculate Conception Mystery that teaches us Mary was without any sin from the first moment of her life. We celebrate the Feast of the Immaculate Conception on December 8.

immersion Method of Baptism that places the person to be baptized completely into the water.

Incarnation The mystery of faith that teaches us God the Son became a human being.

indulgences Removal of all or part of the punishment of purgatory that is granted by the Church for the recitation of certain prayers or the completion of certain devotions or pious practices.

infallible When the pope, in union with the bishops, teaches officially on a matter of revelation, doctrine, or morals, and when this teaching is meant to be believed by the whole Church, he is infallible; he speaks without error, guided by the Holy Spirit.

intercession Form of prayer that asks God for the needs of other people.

knowledge Gift of the Holy Spirit that helps us know all we can about God and our faith.

laity Members of the Church who are not ordained or not members of a religious order.

lectionary Liturgical book of Scripture readings assigned for each Sunday and weekday liturgy. The readings are divided into cycles A, B, and C in the lectionary.

lector Person who reads the Word of God from Scripture to the assembly at a liturgy.

liturgy The public worship of God, the work of Jesus Christ and his Church.

Liturgy of the Eucharist The second part of the Mass, when the bread and wine become the Body and Blood of Christ.

Liturgy of the Word The first part of the Mass, when we hear the Word of God from Scripture.

Matrimony Sacrament of service in which a man and woman vow to live together as husband and wife forever.

Glossary

Messiah The long-awaited Savior. The word means "God's anointed one."

modesty Virtue of guarding personal dignity, especially sexual dignity.

monstrance Ornate container that displays the Blessed Sacrament.

moral decisions Choices between right and wrong.

mortal sin A complete turning away from God. For a sin to be mortal, it must be a very serious offense. The person must know it is seriously wrong and must freely choose to commit this sin.

mysteries of faith Teachings of our faith that we believe but cannot fully understand or explain.

natural law Law found inside each person that lets us know what is right and wrong.

New Testament The second section of the Bible that contains 27 books, including the Gospels, Letters, the Acts of the Apostles, and the Book of Revelation.

obedience Doing what someone else tells one to do. Also, a vow made by religious brothers and sisters to follow the will of the Church and their religious community.

oil of catechumens Oil used to anoint those to be baptized.

Old Testament The first section of the Bible, with 46 books that Christians believe all point forward to Jesus.

one A characteristic of the Church. We are all one family of believers who worship one God.

original sin The sin of Adam and Eve, who used their free will to disobey God. This sin is inherited by each human being.

particular judgment Judgment of each individual person at the moment of death.

Paschal mystery Mystery of faith that tells how Jesus suffered, died, was buried, and rose again to save us from our sins.

penance A prayer or action done to make up for one's sins.

Penance and Reconciliation The sacrament of healing in which a person receives absolution and forgiveness of sins.

Pentecost Sunday The day the Holy Spirit descended upon the apostles. The "birthday of the Church."

petition The form of prayer in which we ask for the things we need, beginning with forgiveness.

piety Gift of the Holy Spirit that helps us truly love and worship God. It is also called reverence.

poverty Owning little property. Also, a vow made by religious brothers and sisters to own no personal property.

praise A form of prayer that glorifies God just because he is God.

priest A man ordained to the second degree of Holy Orders to celebrate Mass, forgive sins, and serve the Church as a teacher and leader.

purgatory A time of purification and suffering after we die until we can be with God forever.

purificator Strip of cloth used to wipe the chalice and ciborium.

reparation Action taken to make up for something one has done wrong.

reputation A person's good name.

restitution The return of something stolen or the repayment of its value.

Resurrection Jesus Christ's greatest miracle, his rising from the dead. Also, the rising of all the dead at the end of the world.

revelation God's divine plan to communicate to us about himself gradually over thousands of years until his final revelation in his Son, Jesus.

Rite of Christian Initiation of Adults (RCIA) Time of study and prayer for older children and adults who want to receive the sacraments of initiation and become members of the Catholic Church.

sacrament A visible, or outward, sign of God's love, given to the Church by Jesus so her members receive God's grace.

sacramentals Outwards signs of God's grace, instituted by the Church.

sacraments of service The two sacraments that bless people for special tasks: Holy Orders and Matrimony.

sacraments of healing The two sacraments that bring us healing: Penance and Reconciliation and Anointing of the Sick.

sacraments of initiation The three sacraments that make us members of the Church: Baptism, Confirmation, and Eucharist.

sacristy Room near the altar where the ministers of the liturgy put on their vestments and where the supplies needed for the liturgy are kept.

Sanctifier One who makes holy. The Holy Spirit is our Sanctifier.

sanctuary lamp Lamp or candle near the tabernacle that is kept lit at all times.

scandal The deliberate leading of another person into evil.

seder A traditional meal with special foods and prayers eaten by Jewish people during Passover.

Son The Second Person in the Holy Trinity. The Son is God, whose mission is to be our Savior.

soul The part of each person that will never die. The soul is a spirit and cannot be seen.

sponsor In Confirmation, the person who stands next to the one being confirmed to show support and to signify the entire Christian community.

steward A trusted servant who cares for another person's property. We are the stewards of God's creation.

tabernacle Special cabinet in a church building that is set apart to hold the Eucharist.

Ten Commandments A "path of life" that shows us through ten laws how to love God and other people. Also known as the Decalogue.

thanksgiving A form of prayer thanking God for all the blessings of our life.

Theotokos Greek title for Mary, meaning "Mother of God."

transubstantiation The doctrine that the bread and wine are changed into the Body and Blood of Christ during the consecration at the Eucharistic Liturgy.

understanding Gift of the Holy Spirit that helps us grasp the meaning of the truths of our faith.

venial sin A less serious sin that does not cut us off from God's life but weakens us.

vice Habitual sin.

virtue Habitual good actions.

vow Solemn promise made to God.

wisdom Gift of the Holy Spirit that helps us make wise decisions that keep God first in our lives.

Saints

We look to canonized saints and holy men and women as models of service to others.

St. Peter Chanel

Feast day April 28
Canonized 1954
Patron of Oceania

St. Peter Chanel was born to a peasant family in France in the early 1800s. He was a bright young man and showed much promise in the field of education. A friend, who was also the parish priest, helped him enter the seminary. After his time of formation, he became a parish priest and remained there for three years. His heart, however, was in the missions. He applied to the Society of Mary (or Marists) and was accepted. He taught in its seminary for five years and then was sent to the missions in the New Hebrides in the South Pacific.

On an island named Futuna, he served the people by healing the sick and working with the native people. The island's heat, the impossible language, and working with tribes that still believed in cannibalism made missionary work in this area a great challenge. For five years, Peter worked joyfully and courageously. When the son of the tribal chief came to Peter to be baptized, the chief was so angered that he had Peter clubbed to death.

What do you find to be the biggest challenge in living your faith?

St. Alphonsus Liguori

Feast day August 1
Canonized 1839
Patron of confessors, theologians, and vocations

St. Alphonsus grew up in Italy and received both a doctorate in civil law and one in canon (Church) law before the age of seventeen! He practiced law for several years and then decided to become a priest. He joined a religious group called the Oratorians. Later he met Sr. Mary Celeste and was impressed by her ideas for a new religious order for women (the Redemptorines). Based upon this rule, he founded an order for men called the Congregation of the Most Holy Redeemer (the Redemptorists). This order was dedicated to preaching and teaching in the poorest areas of the city and country.

St. Alphonsus is one of the doctors of the Church. This title has been granted to fewer than 35 saints and recognizes their great learning, courage, and faithfulness.

Can you name any other doctors of the Church?

St. Gregory the Great

Feast day September 3
Patron of teachers, scholars, musicians, and singers

Have you ever heard that an official title for the pope is *servus servorum Dei?* That is Latin for "servant of the servants of God." St. Gregory is responsible for that term. At a time when the position of pope was often sought for political prestige, Gregory championed the papacy as a position of service.

As a young man, Gregory turned his familial home into a monastery dedicated to St. Andrew. He served there as a humble monk for several years. Later he was ordained and served as a papal ambassador to Constantinople. Then, in 590, he was declared pope, after Pope Pelagius died of the plague. His fifteen years as pope brought many reforms and advances. He is also responsible for the advancement of the Church in England at this time. Gregory was an excellent leader because he always recognized God as the source and goal of his life.

What are some of your goals in life?

St. Margaret Mary Alacoque

Feast day October 1
Canonized 1920

St. Margaret Mary Alacoque is one of the great visionaries of the Church. It is largely because of her that we have the image of the Sacred Heart of Jesus and the devotions related to that image.

Margaret Mary grew up in France and went to the school of the Poor Clares. When she was only ten, she contracted rheumatic fever and became bedridden until she was fifteen. During these years, she developed a close devotion to the Blessed Sacrament. She entered the Visitation religious order when she was 21.

From the age of twenty, she experienced visions of Christ. Most people did not believe her. She said that Christ instructed her to spread the devotion to the Sacred Heart. She persisted against much opposition. Through her tireless efforts, her community began observing the Feast of the Sacred Heart and built a chapel dedicated to the Sacred Heart. Pope Clement XIII officially recognized and approved these devotions 75 years after Margaret Mary's death.

What devotion to Jesus or Mary interests you?

Saints

St. Isaac Jogues, St. John de Brebeuf, and Companions

Feast day October 19
Canonized 1930
Patrons of Canada

St. Isaac, St. John, and their companions served as missionaries to the Huron tribes here in North America. Missionary work at that time was particularly difficult and dangerous, but these men were determined to bring the Word of God to the New World. They were accepted among the Huron and served them for several years. The Iroquois, however, who were enemies of the Huron, thought these "black robes" were responsible for death and evil among the tribes. Even after they were tortured, enslaved, and crippled by the Iroquois, they repeatedly returned to continue preaching God's message of salvation. These men eventually met their deaths as martyrs for the faith.

What sacrifices are you willing to make for your faith?

St. Marie Marguerite d'Youville

Feast day December 23
Canonized 1990

St. Marie Marguerite faced many bad experiences with people in her lifetime. She was born and educated in Canada. Her father died when she was very young. Her mother remarried and because of the reputation of her stepfather, her whole family was shunned by the people of her town. Frances met and married a handsome man who turned out to be a rogue and a gambler. Her mother-in-law criticized her, and when her husband died, she was left with tremendous debts.

Still Marie Marguerite had faith. She used her talents in needlecrafts to start a business and shared her profits with the poor. She gathered other generous women and founded the Sisters of Charity (Grey Nuns) to aid the sick and orphaned.

How do you think St. Marie Marguerite kept her spirits up?

St. Andrew Dung-Lac and Companions

Feast day November 24
Canonized 1988

St. Andrew Dung-Lac is one of 96 Vietnamese martyrs beatified between 1900 and 1951. He was a parish priest who worked in Vietnam during the late 1800s. The history of Vietnam, particularly of Catholicism there, is one of persecution and sacrifice. Permanent missions were opened in the mid-1600s but soon met political resistance, and Catholics who wished to practice their faith were forced into hiding. Several persecutions, under several political leaders, brought martyrdom to over 117 people between 1615 and 1862. One of the martyrs of these Vietnamese persecutions was only nine years old! It is only in this century that Catholicism has been free to grow and progress. Vietnamese Catholics today appreciate and are dedicated to their faith.

What about your faith do you take most for granted?

St. Teresa Benedicta of the Cross (Edith Stein)

Canonized 1998

Edith Stein is considered one of the Catholic martyrs of this century. She was beatified by Pope John Paul II in 1987 and canonized on October 11, 1998.

Edith was born to a large Jewish family in Poland in 1891. She became interested in the Catholic faith and was baptized in 1922. She entered the Discalced Carmelite convent in Cologne, Germany, just before World War II. Because of her Jewish heritage, it was dangerous for her to stay in Germany, so she was sent to a Carmelite convent in Holland. Still, this did not prove to be a safe haven for long. Eventually, she and her sister, Rosa, were arrested and sent to Auschwitz, the infamous Nazi death camp. She was put to death in the gas chambers of that camp in 1942. She was 51 years old.

What does the word "discalced" mean?

Sacred Sites

Sacred sites are places you may visit or think about to help you grow closer to God.

Your Own Prayer Space

Do you have a special place where you feel comfortable praying? Some people will be drawn to nature, the seaside, a garden, the mountains, or the desert. Jesus himself spent prayer time in all these places. Jesus was a man of the outdoors.

Do you feel most prayerful when you are in a church, chapel, cathedral, or quiet room? Jesus, too, went to the Temple and synagogue to pray. Jesus was a man of formal prayer.

Is your prayer most enriching when you are working to help the poor, spending time with a sick friend, visiting someone who is lonely, comforting someone who is frightened, or providing food or shelter for those in need? The Gospels tell us that Jesus invested much of his time in these activities and always blessed his heavenly Father for the ability and the privilege to do so. Jesus was a man of community action.

It is sometimes easy to get lost in good works and not find time to quietly rest in God and listen for direction. Sometimes, we can spend so much time alone on a mountain top praying that we forget that Jesus also spent a great deal of time in the valley with fishermen, lepers, tax collectors, scribes, Pharisees, those who were crippled, blind, and in pain. We may also get so tied up in working with those in need that we don't take time to connect to a community of believers that can serve as support and guidance. It is also easy to do good deeds and feel great about the fact that we are helping. We need to ask, however, is this prayer or the need to boost our own self-esteem? True prayer is a relationship with and connection to the source and reason for all these activities.

Do you know what all this means? It means that *any place you pray is a good place to pray.* Just be sure that you are praying. Another consideration is that you keep a balance. There is a time for private prayer, a time for communal prayer, and a time for social action. We need to recognize the subtle differences. It is most important that you spend some time on your relationship with God.

Where is your favorite place to pray?

Food Pantries and Soup Kitchens

You may not realize that most soup kitchens and food pantries also serve as counseling areas where people who are in need get access to health care, employment opportunities, and housing. These places are the entry to a much larger network of social service agencies and government programs.

The people who work in these facilities are very aware of the sacredness of each person and try to guard the dignity and privacy of each client. The task becomes very difficult because the staff and volunteers also need to be available and aware of the deeper needs of each client and try to address those needs appropriately.

This service is complicated by an intricate combination of federal, state, and local laws and regulations and larger health concerns. God grants knowledge, skills, and special gifts to those he calls into this service. There is one woman who stands out as a guide for all those who feel called to this ministry. Her name is Dorothy Day.

Ask someone to help you find out about Dorothy Day.

Basilica of the National Shrine of the Immaculate Conception, Washington, D.C.

Did you know that Mary, under her title Our Lady of the Immaculate Conception, is the patron of the United States? Did you know that there is a large basilica in Washington, D.C., dedicated to her? A half million pilgrims visit each year to experience the beauty and wonder of this national shrine, which is also the eighth largest church in the world.

There are 38 chapels, oratories, and altars in the upper church alone. There are 36 more in the lower church. Fifty-nine of these chapels are dedicated to Mary. Many chapels reflect the ethnic diversity of our country.

The shrine was built in stages over many years. The foundation stone of the crypt church was laid in 1920. The great upper church did not see its beginnings until 1953 and was dedicated in 1959. The shrine is constantly growing and developing. A spectacular wall sculpture 50 feet wide by 17 feet high entitled, "The Universal Call to Holiness," is set for completion soon.

You might never get to travel to Europe to see the magnificent Old World cathedrals and basilicas. Still, here within your reach is a Catholic shrine to equal and even surpass the beauty of many of her European counterparts.

Can you find out more about this American national shrine?

Sacred Sites

California Missions

If you live in California or near-by states, you probably know about the beautiful mission areas that have been established all along the coast. If you live somewhere else, these missions are great places to visit. Altogether there were 21 missions set up by the Franciscans along the California coast. Nine of these missions were established by one man, Junipero Serra.

Between 1769 and 1782, Fr. Serra was ministering to the Native Americans and settlers in California. Fr. Serra was a Franciscan missionary who was sent into the territory we now know as California. Though Fr. Serra had a leg injury that caused him much pain and disability, his efforts to bring Christianity to the native population of the area never ceased.

Fr. Serra opened and helped develop nine missions and the Presidio Chapel at Monterey. His first mission was opened in 1769 and was called San Diego de Alcala. After that, year after year, moving along the coast, he began new ventures. These included the Presidio Chapel of San Carlos de Borromeo in Monterey (1770), Mission San Carlos de Borromeo in Carmel (1771), Mission San Antonio de Padua (1771), Mission San Gabriel Arcangel (1771), Mission San Luis Obispo de Tolosa (1772), Mission San Francisco de Asis (1776), Mission San Juan Capistrano (1776), Mission Santa Clara de Asis (1777), and Mission San Buenaventura (1782). Fr. Serra died only two years after the building of this final mission.

These missions were originally opened to help the Native Americans learn academic subjects as well as practical skills like farming and raising livestock. They were also places concerned with overall development. Social skills, art, and religion were also taught at the missions. Today, they are noted as places of history, beauty, and prayer.

The missions are beautiful in their Spanish architectural style. The gardens and worship areas in several of these missions look just the way they would have in Fr. Serra's day. The world outside is very different. Yet, when one steps inside the walls of the mission church, time is suspended, and the visitor gets a sense of the bygone era.

Can you find out more about Fr. Serra or the other twelve missions?

Prayers & Practices

Prayers and sacred practices are ways we communicate with God. When we pray, we offer God our praise, adoration, thanksgiving, petition, reparation for sins, and intercession for others' needs. We also observe times of silence in order to listen to God in the quiet of our hearts.

We pray throughout the day.

You have already learned about the Divine Office, also called the Liturgy of the Hours. In the morning, along with other prayers, we pray verses, known as the Canticle of Zechariah, from Scripture. In the evening, we pray the Canticle of the Blessed Virgin Mary, also called the Magnificat. These prayers are prayed daily by all priests and religious men and women. You can join your prayers with theirs each day.

The Canticle of Zechariah

Blessed be the Lord, the God of Israel;
he has come to his people and set them free.

He has raised up for us a mighty savior,
born of the house of his servant David.

Through his holy prophets he promised of old
　　that he would save us from our enemies,
　　from the hands of all who hate us.

He promised to show mercy to our fathers
and to remember his holy covenant.

This was the oath he swore to our father Abraham:
to set us free from the hands of our enemies,
free to worship him without fear,
holy and righteous in his sight
　　all the days of our life.

You, my child, shall be called the prophet of the Most
　　High;
for you will go before the Lord to prepare his way,
to give his people knowledge of salvation
by the forgiveness of their sins.

In the tender compassion of our God
the dawn from on high shall break upon us,
to shine on those who dwell in darkness and the
　　shadow of death,
and to guide our feet into the way of peace.

Prayers & Practices

The Magnificat

My soul proclaims the greatness of the Lord,
my spirit rejoices in God my Savior
for he has looked with favor on his lowly servant.

From this day all generations will call me blessed:
the Almighty has done great things for me,
and holy is his name.

He has mercy on those who fear him
in every generation.

He has shown the strength of his arm,
he has scattered the proud in their conceit.

He has cast down the mighty from their thrones,
but lifted up the lowly.

He has filled the hungry with good things,
and the rich he has sent away empty.

He has come to the help of his servant Israel
for he has remembered his promise of mercy,
the promise he made to our fathers,
to Abraham and his children forever.

Grace Before Meals

Bless us, O Lord, and these your gifts,
which we are about to receive, from your goodness.
Through Christ our Lord.
Amen.

Grace After Meals

We give you thanks for all your gifts,
almighty God,
living and reigning now and for ever.
Amen.

We have many avenues that assist us on our faith journey.

The Seven Sacraments
Baptism
Eucharist
Confirmation
Penance and Reconciliation
Anointing of the Sick
Matrimony
Holy Orders

**The Four Marks
of the Church**
One
Holy
Catholic
Apostolic

Gifts of the Holy Spirit
Wisdom
Understanding
Counsel (right judgment)
Fortitude (courage)
Knowledge
Piety (reverence)
Fear of the Lord (awe and wonder)

Corporal Works of Mercy

Feed the hungry.
Give drink to the thirsty.
Clothe the naked.
Shelter the homeless.
Visit the sick.
Visit those in prison.
Bury the dead.

Spiritual Works of Mercy

Warn the sinner.
Teach the ignorant.
Counsel the doubtful.
Comfort the sorrowing.
Bear wrongs patiently.
Forgive all injuries.
Pray for the living and the dead.

The Beatitudes

Blessed are the poor in spirit, for theirs is the kingdom of heaven.
Blessed are those who mourn, for they shall be comforted.
Blessed are the meek, for they shall inherit the earth.
Blessed are those who hunger and thirst for righteousness, for they shall be satisfied.
Blessed are the merciful, for they shall obtain mercy.
Blessed are the pure in heart, for they shall see God.
Blessed are the peacemakers, for they shall be called children of God.
Blessed are those who are persecuted for the sake of righteousness, for theirs is the kingdom of heaven.

We observe special seasons and practices throughout the year.

Our Church year begins with Advent.

As you know, Advent is a time of preparation. It encompasses four weeks before the celebration of Christmas. We have no way of knowing the exact date of Jesus' birth. Early Christians, however, did know that around December 21 they experienced the shortest day of the year. Immediately after that time, they experienced the days becoming longer and longer. Thus, the ancient people had feasts that celebrated the coming of the light. Since Christians believed that Jesus was the light of the world, what more appropriate time to celebrate his birth?

Lent—40 days or more?

You have always learned that Lent commemorates the 40 days that Jesus spent praying in the desert before his public ministry. If, however, you count the days from Ash Wednesday to Easter Sunday, you'll realize there are actually 46 days! What? Yes, there are 46 days between Ash Wednesday and Easter. Because each Sunday of the year, however, is a grand celebration and commemoration of the resurrection of Jesus, we don't count them in the 40 days of penance. There are six Sundays between Ash Wednesday and Easter Sunday. So, by subtraction, we are left with 40 days.

Why does Easter fall on a different day each year?

In the early days of our Church, just as today, there were many different beliefs. The society was very agricultural, and many religions used the seasons to celebrate special feasts. It was important, in teaching about Jesus, to have people connect the Gospel message to their daily lives. Since Jesus' resurrection was the beginning of a whole new life and occurred so near the spring feasts, it was determined that Easter would always be calculated as the first Sunday after the first full moon after the vernal equinox (that is, the first day of spring).

Holy Days of Obligation (in the United States)

January 1	Feast of the Motherhood of Mary
40 days after Easter	Feast of the Ascension of Our Lord
August 15	Feast of the Assumption of the Blessed Virgin Mary
November 1	Feast of All Saints
December 8	Feast of the Immaculate Conception
December 25	Feast of Christmas

We *fast* and *abstain* from eating meat as a sign of penance.

The season of Lent is a time in which we do penance and prepare ourselves for the wonder of Easter. We pray more. We make a greater effort to financially help those in need. (This is called *almsgiving*.) We make special efforts to make amends for our sinfulness (penance), and we curb our physical desires by restricting our intake of food.

Fasting means that we eat only *one full meatless meal* and two smaller meals with no snacking between meals. This obligation is applied on Ash Wednesday (the beginning of Lent) and Good Friday. This law applies to Catholics aged 21-59.

Abstinence means that we eat *no meat (including poultry) or meat by-products*. We observe abstinence from meat on Ash Wednesday and all Fridays of Lent. This regulation applies to all Catholics over the age of 14.

People who are ill or have particular medical conditions, and women who are pregnant, are not obligated to observe these regulations. Of course, people in these circumstances are urged to pray, do penance, and help the less fortunate as a sign of their repentance and sorrow.

Answer Key

Lesson 1 Activity
Answers will vary.

Lesson 2 Activity
1. most Holy Trinity
2. God, separated
3. Blessed
4. mission
5. holy
6. earth, how

Message: God remains a mystery beyond words.

Lesson 3 Activity

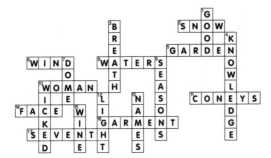

Lesson 4 Activity

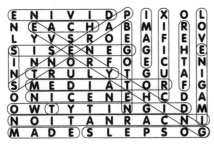

Hidden Message: Only Son of God.

Lesson 5 Activity
1. E   6. H
2. D   7. B
3. I   8. F
4. G   9. C
5. A

Lesson 6 Activity
Answers will vary.

Lesson 7 Activity
1. L   9. C
2. D   10. A
3. J   11. A
4. H   12. H
5. A   13. F
6. B   14. I
7. A   15. E
8. M   16. A

Lesson 8 Activity
Answers will vary.

Lesson 9 Activity
Answers will vary.

Lesson 10 Activity
1. Jesus Christ
2. hierarchy
3. Peter, infallible
4. ecumenical
5. college, pope
6. priests, co-workers
7. deacons, charity

Message: On this rock I will build my Church.

Lesson 11 Activity
Priest: Do justice in workplace

Prophet: Tell others about faith

King: Overcome sin in one's life

Lesson 12 Activity
Sue: obedience

Ben: poverty

Fr. William: obedience

At party: chastity

Fred: obedience and chastity

Beth: poverty

Answer Key

Lesson 13 Activity

She is the Mother of God.

December 8, Mary was conceived without original sin.

Annunciation, angel Gabriel, asked her to be the mother of Jesus.

Mary was a virgin all her life.

While Jesus hung on the cross, he gave Mary to John.

Mary was beneath the cross when Jesus died.

doctrine of the Assumption, Mary is in heaven body and soul now.

She is not God, and Catholics do not pray to her like she is God. They pray in communion with her. They believe Mary can ask God to give them grace.

Lesson 14 Activity

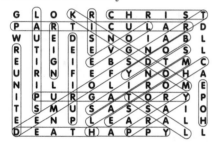

Hidden Message: God will be all in all.

Section One Review

1. False. No new revelation.
2. False. We can still talk about God.
3. True.
4. False. They cannot be separated.
5. True.
6. False. Like us in all things except sin.
7. True.

1. B
2. A
3. B
4. C

5. A
6. B
7. B

Lesson 15 Activity

Answers will vary.

Lesson 16 Activity

1. sacramental
2. sing, minds, God
3. genuflect, tabernacle, sanctuary
4. holy oils
5. holy water

Message: We can meet God through our senses.

Lesson 17 Activity

Lesson 18 Activity

Answers will vary.

Lesson 19 Activity

Answers will vary.

Lesson 20 Activity

Answers will vary.

Lesson 21 Activity

Hidden Message: Our faith is visible and strong.

Lesson 22 Activity
Answers will vary.

Lesson 23 Activity
Answers will vary.

Lesson 24 Activity
1. public, witnesses
2. give, each
3. vows, family
4. priest, deacon
5. covenant

Message: Sign of the new covenant.

Lesson 25 Activity
Answers will vary.

Section Two Review
1. False. Revelation is for us now.
2. True.
3. False. Water also brings death.
4. False. Confirmation completes Baptism.
5. True.
6. False. We are obliged.
7. False. The man and woman give the sacrament to each other.

1. A   5. C
2. A   6. C
3. C   7. B
4. B

Lesson 26 Activity
Answers will vary.

Lesson 27 Activity

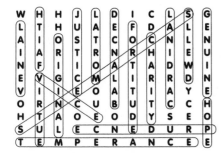

Hidden Message: Which do you choose?

Lesson 28 Activity
Answers will vary.

Lesson 29 Activity
Answers will vary.

Lesson 30 Activity
Answers will vary.

Lesson 31 Activity
Answers will vary.

Lesson 32 Activity
Answers will vary.

Lesson 33 Activity
1. male, female, great
2. commit, adultery
3. covet, wife
4. look, chastity
5. Blessed, pure
6. modest, dignity
7. faithful, never

Message: Thank God for the gift of your body.

Lesson 34 Activity

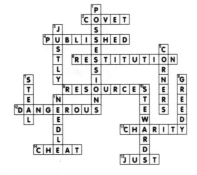

Lesson 35 Activity
Answers will vary.

Answer Key

Section Three Review

1. True.
2. False. The Church speaks to nations.
3. False. All should be given their rights.
4. True.
5. True.
6. False. All people.
7. False. Money is necessary, and we should be poor in spirit.

1. C	5. A
2. A	6. C
3. A	7. B
4. C	

Lesson 36 Activity
Answers will vary.

Lesson 37 Activity

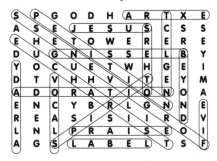

Hidden Message: God has showered you with many blessings.

Lesson 38 Activity

1. model, yes
2. worship, communion
3. John, cross
4. holy, grace
5. sinners, death, eternal

Message: Prayers to Mary are centered on Jesus.

Lesson 39 Activity
Answers will vary.

Section Four Review

1. False. It is real prayer.
2. False. It is for the Church and for each of us personally.
3. True.
4. False. It begins with seeing what we have and blessing God.
5. False. God always blesses us.
6. False. We do not worship Mary.
7. False. All Christians pray the Lord's Prayer.

1. B	5. C
2. A	6. A
3. B	7. A
4. A	